D1084417

ECONOMIC EQUALITY AND FERTILITY
IN DEVELOPING COUNTRIES

ECONOMIC EQUALITY AND FERTILITY IN DEVELOPING COUNTRIES

ROBERT REPETTO

PUBLISHED FOR RESOURCES FOR THE FUTURE
BY THE JOHNS HOPKINS UNIVERSITY PRESS
BALTIMORE AND LONDON

Copyright © 1979 Resources for the Future
All rights reserved
Manufactured in the United States of America

Library of Congress Catalog Card Number 78-20533
ISBN 0-8018-2212-2

Library of Congress Cataloging in Publication Data will be found
on the last printed page of this book.

⡎ CONTENTS

⏚ TABLES AND FIGURES

FIGURES

▌▛ FOREWORD

In 1974 Resources for the Future initiated a program aimed at searching for selective interventions into the development process which would reduce birth rates and hence population growth rates in developing countries. The first product of that program was a collection of essays reviewing what was known about the linkages between fertility and various possible points of intervention, such as education, health care, female-employment opportunities, and improvements in family income and its distribution within a country.[1]

In that volume, Julian Simon, who wrote the chapter on income, found that much of the evidence linking fertility to personal income was of questionable value for policy purposes. The short-run effects of increased income on fertility appear to be positive, and the long-run effects, while negative, require general development to bring them about. But he also concluded that the nature of the effects is likely to be strongly influenced by the way in which the additional income is generated and distributed; and the little evidence then available suggested that there might well be a positive linkage between fertility and equality.

Such a linkage raises intriguing policy implications. If the effect were strong, it would provide an important additional argument for focusing development programs on the poor; that is, a dollar spent in that direction would do more to reduce population growth rates than a dollar spent on across-the-board development. Moreover, it suggests that the alleged incompatibility between egalitarian policies and rapid economic develop-

[1] Ronald G. Ridker, ed., *Population and Development: The Search for Selective Interventions* (Baltimore, Md., Johns Hopkins University Press for Resources for the Future, 1976).

xiii

ment may be incorrect. For if redistribution reduces population growth rates, the reduced dependency burden and increased output per person is likely to increase aggregate savings and hence investment by more than it reduces the average propensity to save out of a given income.

But this approach may be criticized. The evidence from past studies is weak and, in any event, suggests only a correlation between fertility and equality. Is there reason to believe that a causal relationship lies behind this correlation, one that can be used for policy purposes? Even if the relationship is causal, will it operate with sufficient strength and speed to make it feasible as a policy instrument, considering the profound political repercussions associated with redistribution efforts? In any event, is it not likely, as Simon has argued, that the measures utilized to implement the redistribution are more important than the redistribution itself? We concluded with more questions than answers—but also with a determination to search for some answers.

That search led us to Robert Repetto and, eventually, to this book. By all odds it is the most careful, detailed investigation of these issues that is likely to be available for some time to come. Repetto investigates this complex problem in a variety of settings, in each case applying as much rigorous statistical analysis as he can. In addition, however, he combines this analysis with economic, sociological, and historical materials to strengthen and explain the results. He also considers possible ways in which redistributions can be brought about and what they might accomplish both within and among countries, and by so doing he clarifies a number of issues, for example, the effects of land reform.

All the evidence, statistical and historical, gathered both within and among countries, points in the same direction: the distribution of income appears to have an impact on fertility, one that ought to be amenable to policy manipulation. One can wish for better data and for experiments with alternative statistical formulations, but by the time one reaches the last chapter, there is a feeling that the accretion of such additional studies is unlikely to alter the basic point. The remaining doubt on my part pertains to a country's ability and willingness to utilize this information.

We are grateful to the International Bank for Reconstruction and Development for their assistance in supporting this project. In addition, to its financial support, the World Bank helped in the effort to acquire adequate data bases for the analysis; and through its concern about the persistence of population growth, poverty, and inequities in the development process it provided early stimulus to research on this topic.[2] Financial assistance for this project was made possible by a grant from the Rockefeller Foundation to Resources for the Future.

January 1979   Ronald G. Ridker, Senior Fellow,
                                                 The Renewable Resources Division
                                                 Resources for the Future, Washington, D.C.

[2] *Population Policies and Economic Development: A World Bank Staff Report* (Baltimore, Md., Johns Hopkins University Press for the World Bank, 1974).

ECONOMIC EQUALITY AND FERTILITY
IN DEVELOPING COUNTRIES

1 |ᴦ INTRODUCTION

THE MAIN THEME AND ITS IMPLICATIONS

This book is concerned with two of the most disturbing problems of our time: the rapid rise in population, particularly in the less-developed countries, and the increasing disparity in living standards between the world's poor and its affluent. The severity and scope of these problems need no documentation as they have been described in innumerable books, lectures, and conferences on international issues. More important, they have been the object of an increasingly intensive search for solutions. This book is part of that search.

Neither is it necessary to point out that these problems are related. By limiting the resources available for raising living standards, the more rapid growth of population in low-income countries has been partially responsible for the less rapid increases in per capita income that they have generally experienced. This much is clear despite the uncertainties and controversies which still surround the determinants of economic growth. These uncertainties, although important, are not the central concerns of the research presented here.

This book documents the contribution of economic inequality to rapid population growth through its effect on birth rates. It shows that a more unequal distribution of income within a community implies a higher aggregate birth rate and a faster rate of population growth. This is true for individual nations composed of rich and poor households, and for the world community of rich and poor nations as well. It shows that for a community at any level of economic development, as measured by *average* income per capita or some similar index, the overall birth rate of the community will be lower, the more equally distributed that total income is. Economic inequalities work to maintain high fertility and rapid population growth.

1

Societies in which economic gains are limited to a narrow elite, while the vast majority lead marginal lives of insecurity and deprivation, display high fertility. Any fertility declines under these conditions are usually concentrated within the small fraction of households who have benefited from the economic system. The continuing accrual of income and wealth to the already affluent does little to reduce the rate of population growth in such societies, since they are a numerically small group with relatively low fertility.

Gains in income and the changes in living standards which accompany them have different effects on fertility, according to the initial income levels of the recipients. The relation between fertility and the level of income for most populations above subsistence levels can be described empirically by a U-shaped or backward J-shaped curve. At low levels of income, increases in living standards result in rapid fertility declines. For those within that society in higher ranges of income, increases in income may result in little or no change in fertility. At high-income levels, increases in income may result in some increase in fertility. Consequently, it is impossible to refer generally to the effect of economic improvements on birth rates. The economic status of those who experience the improvement is a key determinant of that effect. The impact of income growth on birth rates depends on who gets the income. In other words, the *distribution* of income matters.

Having babies is the way in which couples try to get the number of children they want, or which their community lets them know they ought to have. In economic jargon, fertility is a stock-adjustment process, by which actual and desired family size are brought into line. At low income levels, economic improvement greatly affects all the elements of this process. Infant mortality rates fall, primarily because infants who are better nourished and cared for can better resist the infections and infestations they are subject to. As a result, couples need have fewer children in order to end up with the number they want.

Economic change among low-income households influences the number of children that couples want. Parents pin their hopes for the future to a lesser extent on the chance that one of their children will manage to prosper enough to care for them should the need arise. As the household's income improves, parents rely to a greater extent on their own accumulation of assets or on societal sources of security. Parents perceive opportunities for their children that require an investment in their education. They have the resources with which to provide their children these changes, even at increasing sacrifice to themselves. Parents enter a world in which there are chances to earn and spend money and time outside the family, one in which social standing is determined more by material possessions and life-style than by kinship and community ties. These changes tend to reduce the number of children that couples think are appropriate.

Also, economic gains greatly affect the ability of women and couples to regulate effectively the number and timing of their births. Not only do rising income and education make effective contraception more accessible and acceptable, but the escape from conditions of chronic insecurity and deprivation leads to circumstances in which long-term planning and individual control of important life choices seem more feasible and desirable.

At higher levels of economic well-being, after infant mortality rates have already dropped, after family-size norms have already converged among all population subgroups to a narrow range of two to four children, and after effective contraception has become widely practiced, further increases in income and consumption do little to change actual fertility. The critical changes have already occurred: couples get about the number of children they want, and they do not want many.

The fact that different patterns of income distribution imply different fertility rates for the population as a whole has important implications. For one, it provides a strong reason to doubt the existence of a tradeoff between rapid growth and greater equity in development patterns. It suggests that greater equality in the distribution of benefits from development leads to more rapid increases in income per capita. A more equal distribution of income lowers the rate of population growth by reducing fertility. This permits faster accumulation of capital per worker, including both physical and human capital. This, in turn, promotes faster growth in output per worker. Because of the reduced dependency ratio of nonworkers to workers, resulting from the reduced rate of fertility, even faster growth occurs in output and income per capita. In addition, the reduced dependency ratio and the faster growth of income per capita promotes a higher savings rate. Further, given the limited substitution possibilities between labor and other inputs in aggregate production, the faster growth of the capital stock and the slower growth of the labor force implies an increase in labor's share of total output. Presumably, the consequence of this is a further reduction in the inequality of the size distribution of income. These further reductions sustain the decline in fertility, leading to further increases in income per capita. This sketches a process by which equalization of incomes, decline in fertility, and faster growth in output per capita interact positively. Progress in solving the problem of inequality aids the solution of the problem of population growth, and vice versa. The empirical findings of chapter 2 support this prediction, suggesting a strong positive interaction between income redistribution and fertility decline. A more equal distribution of output, desirable in itself, also leads to faster increases in output per capita through reductions in the rate of population growth.

The fact that the distribution of income substantially affects the fertility rate of a population also has important consequences for policymakers engaged in the search for effective interventions by which to stimulate accelerated fertility decline. Discouraged at the prospects for rapid and general economic growth in the developing countries as the solution to population problems, policymakers have attempted to find selective, short-run interventions which can affect birth rates, even prior to the attainment of development targets by the mass of the population. Subsidized family-planning services, special educational programs for women, and the provision of fiscal incentives and disincentives related to family size reflect this search.

However, income redistribution, and the promotion of more rapid income growth among households in the lower half of the income scale, *are* very selective interventions. In the typical less-developed country, households in the bottom half of the income scale together receive only 15 to 20 percent of total personal income, but they account for three-fourths of all births. At the other extreme, the most affluent 10 percent of households typically may receive 40 or 50 percent of total household income. Increases in the income of these well-off households are largely irrelevant to the process of demographic change. Increases in the income of those in the lower income brackets may be critical. In many less-developed countries, the 15 or 20 percent of personal income accruing to these households is not much larger than the share of national resources devoted to education and health. In this sense, accelerating the improvement in living standards of those whose fertility would be thereby affected is not synonymous with accelerated economic development, but it is every bit as selective as other population interventions. General development is a process by which the lion's share is assigned to the lion: since income distributions change but little under typical development strategies, it can be assumed that the well-off will receive the same share of additional resources which they already enjoy of existing resources. Redirecting resources to those groups who receive little is a selective strategy.

The same is true on the international level. During the development decade of the 1960s, developed countries received more than 80 percent of the increase in world income, slightly more than their share in 1960. This increase in income probably had little to do with the change in fertility in the developed countries during this decade, and certainly almost nothing to do with the change in world fertility, since 85 percent of the births took place in the less-developed countries. From the standpoint of world population growth, all this income growth in the affluent countries was virtually irrelevant.

The findings of this book also open up another avenue of policy intervention. Economists and others interested in ways to promote fertility decline have emphasized interventions to widen access to those services thought to be associated with fertility decline: family-planning services, formal education, and maternal and child-health care are important examples. Their emphasis on the *supply* of such services as a means of promoting fertility reduction is ironic, since their contribution to population research has been to emphasize the importance of the *demand* for children as a determinant of high fertility. The complementarity of these supply-oriented interventions with programs to raise the economic status of low-income and high-fertility households has been missed. In fact, whatever the supply, low-income households are constrained from making use of these services by their lack of means. Even subsidized services often have substantial opportunity costs or other barriers that exclude poor families, who cannot afford to send children to school because they are needed for work at home or because to do so would involve spending for clothes or books; who cannot afford to travel to clinics and wait for appointments, or to buy the medicines that are prescribed.

Whereas poverty forces households to disinvest in their own future by elevating subsistence needs to predominance, improvements in economic welfare at low-income levels substantially raises the demand for education, for health, for improved housing, and for other investments by the family in itself. This is one reason why large families, which are intrinsically poor "investments" in overpopulated societies, are rationalized as being the only hope of future security for poor households. Additional resources provided to such households result in the substitution of other sources of future well-being. The findings of chapters 4 and 5 lend strong support to this generalization. By implication, there are strong complementarities between policies that raise income levels among low-income households and those which increase the supply of basic services to them.

One reason why this complementarity has been largely overlooked has been the belief held by economists that increases in income—especially if they are obtained by methods that do not raise the opportunity cost of children—would result in higher fertility. This belief, although very weakly supported by empirical evidence, stems from the theory of consumer behavior, which contends that "children should not be inferior goods." However, as will be argued in more detail in chapter 2, this theoretical prediction is based on a model of fertility behavior which minimizes the broader effects of improvements in living standards and which treats fertility as a demand-determined process rather than one of stock adjustment. By no means need increases in income have this consequence. Chapter 4 suggests that in the experience of at least one country—Korea —they did not.

THE METHOD AND ORGANIZATION OF THE STUDY

This book treats as an hypothesis the basic argument that fertility is affected by the distribution of income and organizes evidence to provide the most decisive tests possible of the null hypothesis: that it is *not*. Far more emphasis is placed on devising conclusive tests of the thesis than on elucidating all of the possible ways in which income distribution might influence fertility. Consequently, much attention is paid to formal hypothesis testing. To some, the argument may seem to be narrow, lacking in sociological and economic breadth and, possibly, depth. Part of the reason for this may be that the research effort has been directed deliberately toward the discovery of a minimal set of sufficient conditions which would establish or refute the hypothesis, and the empirical test of those conditions. The methodological approach and the findings of this book are sufficient to show that the distribution of income affects fertility. They do not explore in depth all the ways in which this influence is exerted, although in successive chapters increasing attention will be devoted to the exploration of these channels of influence.

Another aim of this book is that of demonstrating the implications of demographic facts which have long been known and accepted. The fact, for example, that the relationship of fertility to income and related economic status variables is roughly U-shaped has been well-known for a long time, but its implications with regard to the distribution of income have not been brought out. The tests and procedures used in this study can readily be extended to other kinds of data, and existing demographic data can easily be reinterpreted to bear on this thesis.

Chapter 2 presents a simplified conceptual framework from which sufficient tests of the hypothesis are derived. It will be demonstrated that a sufficient condition and a key test is that the response of a household's fertility to changes in its income per capita is an increasing function of income. The conceptual framework for this is that fertility is a stock-adjustment process. This integrates a number of previously unrelated insights about the determinants of fertility. However, this particular framework is by no means a necessary one for the derivation of the hypothesis. Other theories can lead to the same conclusion. In this sense, the hypothesis that the distribution of income affects fertility is *robust*: it is implied by many models of household behavior. The null hypothesis, that the distribution of income of a population has no affect on its birth rate, is shown to be the special case.

The book will present a number of empirical tests of this hypothesis, each representing a different perspective and a different kind of evidence. The earlier chapters will build up this evidence into an increasingly comprehensive set of tests. The first of these, the results of which are also presented in chapter 2, uses aggregative data from a cross-national sample, characterized by very different degrees of income concentration, income levels, and fertility rates. Here, the emphasis will be on the interaction of income distribution and fertility. The kind of evidence employed has its special limitations, but it permits analysis of the long-run effects of substantial and persistent differences in the degree of inequality among populations. The results clearly reject the null hypothesis, and point toward a strong positive interaction between greater income equality and lower fertility rates.

Chapter 3 constructs an alternative test, using disaggregated data from a large sample of individual households. The data refer to Puerto Rican families in 1970. In chapter 3 emphasis is on the response of household fertility to changes in household income per capita, at different income levels. The idea that household fertility is a stock-adjustment process will be tested directly as well. The evidence strongly supports the hypothesis that the response of household fertility to changes in household income is income-dependent and rises substantially with the level of income per capita. This is another confirmation of the importance of income distribution to population fertility rates. Equally strong support will be found for the stock-adjustment fertility model. Additional empirical tests discriminate among the thesis of this book and other related hypotheses, especially the hypothesis that the fertility of the household is affected by its relative economic status.

Chapter 4 is a case study of economic development and fertility change in the Republic of Korea. It will provide an historical and longitudinal perspective on the consequences of income redistribution. In South Korea, the redistribution of income arose largely from exogenous influences: wartime destruction, hyperinflation, land and educational reform triggered by the U.S. occupational force and the pressure of the Communist influence in the North. This isolates the experience from the interactive mechanisms that are explored in chapter 2 and from the confounding influence of other policy orientations, since subsequent economic policy in Korea was not redistributive either in intent or in effect. The case study explores the mechanisms of influence in substantially greater depth. It finds as one consequence of the absence of socioeconomic stratification the rapid diffusion of changes in marriage patterns, fertility norms, abortion, and contraceptive practice throughout Korean society with relatively few lags or differentials. This stands in marked contrast to the pattern of fertility change in more highly stratified societies, in which wide fertility differentials between the advantaged and disadvantaged open up and persist over long periods.

Chapter 4 also finds little to support the presumption that increases in household wealth lead to higher fertility. The Korean land reform, which made small proprietors of millions of Korean tenants, and the subsequent rise in urban and rural land values, seems rather to have provided households with an alternative asset and source of long-term security, at the same time that the increase in educational and occupational opportunities substantially raised both the costs and returns on investments in children's education.

The case study concludes with a formal econometric analysis of current Korean fertility based on data from a large sample of Korean households. This analysis extends that of chapter 3 by showing some of the mechanisms through which economic changes affect fertility—through changes in marriage and contraceptive practice, as well as through attitudes toward family size, the education of children, and the source of old-age security. The results strongly reinforce both the historical findings and those derived from the Puerto Rican study. There is a nonlinear relationship between income and fertility in Korea which arises directly and also indirectly from the effect of income on intermediate variables, notably the aspirations of parents to invest in their children's education.

These three chapters build up a body of evidence—aggregative, disaggregated, and historical—bearing on the main thesis. The evidence consistently supports it. Chapter 5 will cover the means of redistribution in a developing society. Based on a region of rural India, the study explores the determinants of the existing distribution of income and the mechanisms for change. As have so many other investigations before, the study concludes that the distribution of land—the main asset and source of power in a rural community—is the primary determinant of the distribution of income; and that any successful program of redistribution in such rural communities must include a redistribution of land ownership as a main element.

The final chapter, chapter 6, applies the same arguments and empirical tests to world fertility and the world distribution of income. The findings demonstrate that greater equality in the distribution of world income would lower world fertility for the same reasons that apply within nations. From the demographic standpoint, the overwhelmingly large share of the growth in world income which has accrued to the already-rich countries has been ineffective. The small share of world resources which have gone to the low-income countries have been much more important in promoting declines in world fertility. The world's poor, the low-income households of low-income countries, receive a strikingly small proportion of total world income, whatever the problems of measurement and comparability. The inevitable conclusion is that changes in policies in both rich and poor countries which would raise living standards in poor countries would lead to a substantial decline in world fertility and in the rate of population increase. It is shown that, given the characteristics of the world's poor and the structure of the economies in which most of them live, international policies to accelerate the growth of employment are the main avenues, outside of direct resource transfers, toward significant improvement in world income distribution and the situation of the poor.

THE LIMITATIONS OF THE STUDY

The subject matter of this book demands great understanding of societal processes. The means which could be employed in this study are meager relative to the requirements of the task. The limitations in the concepts underlying the research and in the use of data are keenly felt. Much remains to be better understood.

There is an obvious need for investigating the interaction of economic and demographic change at the level of the household. Unfortunately, there are few adequate sources of information which follow households through long periods of time in developing countries. Panel studies and resurveys of previously studied populations could provide the necessary raw materials for such work.

It is also clear that additional research is required in order to investigate more directly the impact on fertility of policies and programs which have the effect of redistributing income or raising the economic conditions of low-income households. An adequate base for policy formulation can rarely be created without pilot operations, experimental programs, or evaluations of past and present activities. In any developing society, there is a feasible set of interventions, probably not very large, which would have a substantial impact on the welfare of low-income households. To date, there has been almost no evaluation or direct investigation of the impact of such programs on fertility or on other demographic processes. Unless a wait of a decade is acceptable before we can judge the impact of programs now under way, such research can only be carried out by constructing adequate, retrospective quasi-experimental designs.

2 ▐▐▐ THE CONCEPTUAL FRAMEWORK AND EVIDENCE FROM AGGREGATED DATA

THE CONCEPTUAL FRAMEWORK

The idea that the onset of a broad fertility decline is associated with the exposure of a substantial fraction of the population to modern systems of social, economic, and value organizations has extensive antecedents in the "threshold hypothesis," which was popular in the 1950s and 1960s (United Nations, 1963). From this idea several authors have inferred that development strategies which promote the participation of the largest possible fraction of the population in the process of modernization will lead to the most rapid reductions in birth rates (Kocher, 1974; and Rich, 1973). Rich has succinctly stated this idea:

The shift in attitude toward reduced birth is, rather, a function of environmental changes that affect the orientation of families enough to alter fertility decisions. In a developing country, this appears to occur when families begin to participate significantly in modern social, political and economic systems. Thus, nations in which only a small elite constitutes the modern sector while the majority of the population continues to live at the subsistence level and to maintain its traditional way of life are not likely to experience reduced national fertility as readily as those countries which bring about mass participation in the development process. [Rich, 1973, page 9]

From this idea it is not far to the hypothesis that the distribution of income within a country will influence its fertility rate. The missing step is only the recognition that in order to hold modern attitudes and to behave in a modern way, it is necessary that people participate in modern systems, and that if they do so, they will acquire the corresponding attitudes and behavior patterns (Inkeles and Smith, 1974). Participation in

11

modern life, or even the sustained aspiration to participate, requires that people have the means to partake of a variety of consumption activities, to invest in themselves and their children, to be concerned with more than day-by-day subsistence, and to come in contact with a broader range of experience. Conversely, rising living standards draw people into contact with a wider range of modern systems from which they had been effectively excluded by poverty. In other words, within certain ranges at least, rising income levels might be both necessary and sufficient for the process of modernization underlying fertility declines. This notion is fully consistent with the idea that among households *within* the modern sector and those already extensively participating in modern socioeconomic systems, changes in income might play a weak or even reversed role in inducing fertility changes (Gregory and Campbell, 1976). The narrowing of fertility differentials by income and other socioeconomic characteristics that occur as modernization is diffused throughout a society suggests that this may be the case.

These broad arguments are inadequate as a conceptual framework for research, because they leave indefinite the mechanisms by which income and its distribution affect fertility. Unfortunately, there is no complete theory of fertility. Instead, there are a number of partial models which emphasize particular determinants. Social scientists study fertility change as blind men study the elephant, seizing on some part of the whole. The simple explanations of the past—urbanization, industrialization, and declining infant mortality rates—have given way to a new generation of simple explanations—the declining value of children, the changing status of women, and the impact of family-planning programs. Even economists' models of fertility, from which many of these more recent insights have been derived, tend to focus attention on the determinants of demand for children within marital unions, and ignore many other influences on fertility in developing countries.

This chapter does not offer a new general theory of fertility change in developing countries, although it does contain a modest attempt toward integration of existing models. Instead, it focuses on a property which many different theories have in common, one implying that the fertility level of a population is dependent on the distribution of income within it. The hypothesis that the distribution of income is influential in determining population fertility rates stands or falls on the existence of nonlinearities in the relationship between the fertility of individual families and their incomes. This is true because the distribution of income among households can be irrelevant to the overall fertility of the population only if the response of household fertility to a change in household income is the same for all households, regardless of their initial income positions. Otherwise, the effect of a change in income on fertility, for any household, will be affected by the economic position of that household. Consequently, different patterns of income distribution would result in different overall fertility rates for the population as a whole.

In other words, one way in which the thesis of this book can be tested, using household data, is by testing the proposition that the change in fertility, with respect to a change in income dF/dY, is independent of the level of income: that is, $dF/dY = a$, where a is either a constant, possibly zero, or $da/dY = 0$. This implies that household fertility is a linear function of household income over the entire relevant range of household incomes. Otherwise, it is easy to show that the population fertility rate will depend not only on mean income within the population, but also on the higher moments of the distribution of income.

Knowledge of the general relationship underlying this statement first became widely known to economists through efforts to find econometrically testable macroeconomic functions which could be derived from theoretically postulated microeconomic relationships, known as "the aggregation problem." Despite the formal similarity, it should be clear that in this context, the argument has more than statistical significance. For if the response of household fertility to changes in household income differs at different levels, and if the population fertility rate is an important policy variable, then the distribution of income is important as a matter of population policy.

The implications of nonlinearity are so fundamental to this investigation that, at a risk of belaboring the obvious, a simple example will demonstrate the preceding argument. Suppose there is, at the household level, a quadratic relationship between household fertility and income. Let

$$F_i = aY_i + bY_i^2 \tag{2-1}$$

where the subscript i represents the ith household, and F represents the number of births within a given time interval. Then, assuming this holds for income changes experienced by the individual household, $dF_i/dY_i = a + 2bY_i$, which depends on the household's initial income. From individual household period fertility F_i, a population rate can be formed by aggregating all households and dividing by the appropriate number of women:

$$1/N\sum_i F_i = F = a(1/N)\sum_i Y_i + b(1/N)\sum Y_i^2 \tag{2-2}$$

The population fertility rate F is seen to depend both on the first and second moments of the population distribution of income. Actually,

$$F = a\bar{Y} + b\bar{Y}^2 + b \operatorname{Var}(Y) \tag{2-3}$$

The population fertility rate depends on mean income and its population variance, a summary measure of the inequality of income. Consequently, the hypothesis can be tested either by using household data and an estimating equation analogous to Equation 2-1, or by using aggregated data and one like Equation 2-3. In fact, if the household behavioral relation is nonlinear in income, a measure of income variance must be included in any empirical relation based on aggregated data, or else the estimated influences of all other variables will generally be biased away from their true values.

The specific fertility effect of differential income changes will depend on the shape of the nonlinear relationship. Figure 2-1 illustrates the point that over some ranges of income, like $Y_0 - Y_1$, a redistribution of income in favor of the relatively poor would raise the aggregate fertility of that population; over other ranges such as $Y_2 - Y_3$, a relative change in favor of households at the low end of the range would lower the aggregate fertility level. Over this range, the fall in fertility among relatively low-income households, as income rises, is greater than the fall (or rise) in fertility in response to a rise in income among higher-income households.

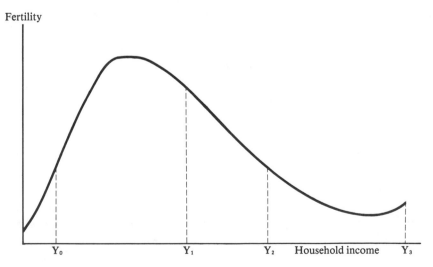

Figure 2-1. Nonlinearity in the income-fertility relation.

That any relationship between fertility and income should be non-linear is intuitively appealing, if only because linearity is an extreme, knife-edge condition which cannot be expected to hold over all ranges of income. Beyond that, such a nonlinear relation has been suggested for several reasons, arising out of interactions between income changes and other determinants of fertility. It has been suggested in the literature on population research that there are interactions between income and urbanization, income and the perceived costs of children, income and the relative preference for children, and income and education. For these and other reasons, Schultz (1974), after summarizing a large body of recent econometric research into the socioeconomic determinants of fertility, has concluded, "Finally, the character of family size suggests that linear models are too restrictive for the study of fertility. Both theoretical and empirical evidence have been presented for non-linearity between explanatory variables and fertility."

Linear models are useful for many purposes, but the exploration of distributional issues is not one of them. In empirical research, most investigations, by specifying relationships to be linear a priori, have ruled out distributional effects. When investigators have admitted possible non-linearities they have generally found them. Typically, the relationship between fertility and household income takes the form of a U or an inverted J. This implies that a more equal distribution is associated with a lower fertility level. These findings have come from cross-sectional disaggregative studies (Ben-Porath, 1973; Bernhardt, 1972; Sanderson and Willis, 1971; Simon, 1974; and Willis, 1973), and also from time-series studies of long-run changes in fertility (Hashimoto, 1974; and Wilkinson, 1973). More recent research which has considered causal linkages running from the level of fertility to the level of household income, as well as the reverse, also comes to the same conclusion (Haut, 1977; and Snyder, 1975).

Further intuitive support for a nonlinear relationship can be derived from a general "stock-adjustment" model of household fertility behavior, in which current fertility acts as a decision variable through which the family tries to bring the actual number of children as nearly into alignment as possible with the number desired by the household at that particular time (Lee, 1977; Schultz, 1977; and Tobin, 1973). In this representation, current fertility is influenced by three main elements: (1) the number of children currently alive in the family, along with their individual characteristics perhaps; (2) the number of children which the family wishes to have, at that moment; and (3) the speed and efficiency with which the couple is able to control its fertility.

The first depends on both random and systematic factors which influence the timing, sex, and viability of births; also, the community and household characteristics which influence the survival probabilities of infants. The second is the result of all those forces which determine the *demand* for children, in the economist's vocabulary. These include not only the economic costs or value of children, household wealth, the opportunity costs of the wife's time spent in child care, and similar economic variables, but also the entirety of psychological and cultural traits which determine the couple's preference and motivation for children. In other words, the relevant forces are those which determine both the constraint set and the preference set. The third, the adjustment factor, subsumes both contraceptive efficiency and fecundity, which together determine the degree to which a couple can alter natural fertility to attain or approximate family-size objectives. A simple stock-adjustment model illustrating the joint effects of these elements is presented in appendix B (page 33).

This representation of the determination of household fertility undoubtedly has its limitations. For example, it is at best a model of marital fertility, although the marital decision is itself an important determinant of fertility (Becker, 1973 and 1974). Yet, despite these limitations, it integrates several strands of theory. Traditional demographic theory has emphasized the supply forces which influence the stock of children alive in the household; for less-developed countries, the salient force is often that of infant mortality. Socioeconomic research has emphasized forces which influence the number of children that couples will want. Economic and sociological theories are complementary, the former stressing opportunity costs and economic constraints, the latter the formation of preferences and family-size norms. It is the interplay of these two which fixes the household's effective demand for children. Both sociologists and economists tend to share the assumption that it is this effective demand which for the most part determines fertility; that the household can produce and sustain the children it wants, and that either the individual household or the broader culture is capable of applying effective regulation of births so that achieved fertility will be broadly in alignment with that desired by the household or considered appropriate by the community.

On the other hand, some sociologists and psychologists, as well as the main body of family-planning programmers, emphasize the importance of the regulatory mechanism itself as a separate and important determinant of fertility. On the grounds that available means of birth control are not adequate to ensure the degree of regulation required to adjust fertility to rapidly changing circumstances, or that an important fraction of couples are mentally or emotionally ill-equipped to apply available contraceptive methods successfully, these observers suggest that variations in the effectiveness of fertility regulation are important sources of variations in fertility (Ryder, 1973).

A simple test of this stock-adjustment is carried out in chapter 3. The model suggests that current fertility, other things being equal, should be influenced—negatively—by the number of living children in the family; that is, the more children, the lower the current fertility. An alternative hypothesis—that fertility differences among women *persist,* either due to differences in fecundity or to differences in the capability of fertility regulation—would lead to the opposite prediction: that current fertility should be associated—positively—with the stock of living children.

In order to link this representation of fertility determination to the discussion of nonlinearity, it is sufficient to observe that all elements of the model are income-related. Infant and child mortality rates fall sharply with improvements in living standards of the household over a range of incomes. There is mounting evidence that this is caused, not by improved access to preventive or curative medical services, but to the host's increased resistance to infectious and parasitic diseases. Also, within some ranges of income, fecundity may respond positively to improvements in living standards. This may be in response to improvements in the nutritional status of mothers (Frisch, 1974) or to the length of postpartum amenorrhea, arising out of changes in breast-feeding (Huffman, Chakraborty, and Moseley, 1977).

On the demand side, long-term increases in income are associated with a host of changes in role expectations, aspirations, values, and household organization which make for lower fertility norms and preferences. Some of these mechanisms are documented for Korean households in chapter 4. Recent sociological research has shown that the perceived financial constraint limiting expected family size is rapidly attenuated with rising income levels (Thornton and Kim, 1977). Moreover, the perceived and actual costs of child-rearing depend strongly on the socioeconomic status of the household, so that opportunity costs are also income-related (Turchi, 1975).

Also, rising economic circumstances result in improvements in the effectiveness of fertility control and in declines in the perceived costs. This stems in part from greater accessibility of contraceptives, lower information costs, and higher educational levels. However, a main change seems to be the heightened sense of personal efficacy and purposefulness which accompanies the escape from poverty into conditions of relative economic security and stability. Poverty is accompanied by constant insecurity and frequent frustration and deprivation. Adaptive attitudinal responses include concern for the present rather than the future; passivity; fatalism; feelings of powerlessness; disbelief in the efficacy of individual effort; and, consequently, poor planning capabilities. Sociological studies have found these to be situational characteristics of low-income households (Askham, 1975). Among the consequences are relatively poor success at birth control, and a high frequency of unintended pregnancies. These are markedly reduced as households approach middle-class status.

Finally, although there is little systematic evidence available, it is likely that higher economic status is accompanied by greater welfare gains from spacing of children, and less tolerance for unintended deviations from family-size goals. Both of these additional factors affect the optimal efficiency of contraception and current fertility rates. Consequently, with all parameters of the model's direct or indirect functions of household income, it is clear that the resulting relationship between fertility and income is not a linear one.

It is not central to the point that these factors are also influenced by other socioeconomic characteristics of the household, like educational status, work participation, and residence, since these are themselves strongly influenced by household living standards, except perhaps in the very short run. The preoccupation of economists with the short-run, *ceteris paribus* effects of income changes on fertility is largely an artifact of economic theories of consumer demand, which suggests that the effect of "pure" income changes on fertility should be positive. However, there is little policy interest in this short-run impact, since sustained improvements in income affect fertility through many channels. What is significant in this context is the presumption of nonlinearity.

Easterlin (1975) used a similar framework to suggest one possible mode of dependence of fertility on income. Although his model is in terms of completed fertility, the underlying conception is similar. In figure 2-2, N represents the expected size of the family. It rises with income, because of declining infant mortality and improving fecundity. N^* represents desired family size, and at low-income levels this may be greater

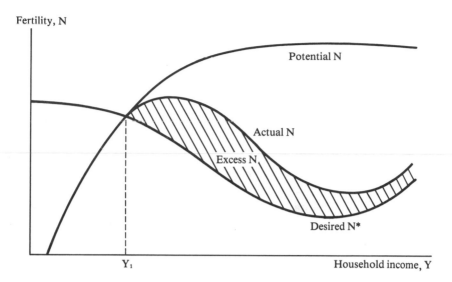

Figure 2-2. A possible source of nonlinearity
in the income-fertility relation.

than that which is expected. N^* may fall substantially over some range
of income, then level off or, indeed, rise because of the positive effect of
wealth. As long as expected fertility is below that desired, it constrains
actual fertility, and motivation to limit births is absent. At income levels
higher than some level Y_1, possible fertility exceeds that desired, and
actual fertility depends on the effectiveness of regulation. As the effectiveness of regulation improves with rising income, the gap between actual
and desired fertility narrows, while the former falls quite sharply. When
actual and desired fertility are brought closely into alignment in a population using contraception effectively, movements in actual fertility will
be governed largely by demand factors, and may level out or rise with
further increases in income. The resulting dependence of fertility on income is highly nonlinear.

While this is but one possible scenario, it is plausible and seems applicable to the behavior of the populations studied in later chapters. However, it should be emphasized that the hypothesis that the distribution of
household income influences fertility within the population is robust, in
the sense that it is implied by a wide variety of theories and models of
household behavior. It is the counterhypothesis, that income distribution
does not influence fertility, which is special.

EVIDENCE FROM AGGREGATIVE DATA

The initial test of the thesis of this book employs data from a cross-national sample of sixty-eight developed and less-developed countries for which observations on all the variables could be taken for a single period in the mid-1960s. Inevitably, the quality of the data varies widely from country to country, and there are some inconsistencies in the definitions or differences in the measurement of certain variables among countries, although care was take to obtain the most consistent set of observations available.

Given these limitations, and the possibility of employing household data, the use of a cross-national sample requires some explanation. The strongest justification is that it permits observation of populations which have been living under very different income distributions for considerable periods of time, and permits an exploration of the long-run effects of differences in income distribution. Within most economies, changes in income distribution tend to be slow, and the effects difficult to distinguish from those of other trendlike variables. A cross-national sample provides wide variation in all the important variables.

Furthermore, the probability that there are substantial errors of measurement in the principal variables does not by any means imply that the validity of the tests of association is weakened. In general, with errors of measurement, any observed association between the variables can be taken as the floor above which the true association in absolute value is likely to lie. The errors of measurement create "noise" which reduces the strength of the association. Measurements of correlation or covariance tend to be biased toward zero. Therefore, if a close association is found to exist in data of poor quality, there is reason to suspect that the true association between the variables is even closer.

This is true, of course, only if the errors of measurement in the different variables are independent across the sample of countries. However, this condition is likely to be fulfilled by measurements of the birth rate and the distribution of income. These statistics are estimated from entirely different sources of information, by independent methodologies, and usually by different agencies. There seems no reason to suspect that if the birth rate is overestimated, the degree of inequality in the distribution of income among households should also be overestimated; and, if the birth rate is underestimated, the inequality in the income distribution should be also.

A similar set of considerations explains the inclusion of both more-developed and less-developed countries in the same sample. One can be sure that the differences in fertility rates, levels of living, and the degree of income inequality between countries at widely different levels of development are not simply, or primarily, errors of measurement. They represent real and systematic differences among those populations. Inclusion of a wide sweep of systematic variation in the variables of interest within the sample permits a more reliable estimation of the relationships of the system. Restriction of the sample, on the other hand, to the less-developed countries alone would tend to increase the "noise" level relative to the true signal. It is well known that the birth rates in less-developed countries have been distributed around a modal value of about 40, and in the more developed countries, about 20. Few would suspect that the intermodal differences represented primarily measurement error. However, the difference between a crude birth rate of 44 in one less-developed country and a measured rate of 41 in another might, indeed, be just a measurement error. It seems obvious that better understanding of the underlying forces determining long-term fertility differentials would be obtained if the broader systematic differences were explored along with the narrower ones, which are taken up subsequently with data from single countries and regions.

The use of aggregative tests requires explicit recognition of the simultaneous interaction of fertility and income distribution. A number of mechanisms have been noted through which the level of fertility might be expected to influence the distribution of income. Some of these have to do with the way in which income distribution is conventionally measured, as the variation in income among all households at a particular date. This has no close relationship to the difference among households in total lifetime income. As both Kuznets (1975) and Paglin (1975) have recently made clear, changes in the age distribution of the population will affect current distribution of income, because of the life cycle of earnings, without necessarily affecting the distribution of lifetime incomes. Lower fertility and mortality rates, by elongating the age pyramid and increasing the variation in age among earners, would tend to increase the current inequality in the distribution of earned income. Other demographic effects on income distribution have been pointed out by Kuznets (1975). The fact that larger households tend to have larger incomes but smaller incomes per household member, gives rise to an important distinction between the distribution of incomes among households and the distribution of a household's income among its individual members. The identity of the poor tends to be masked within the distribution of household income by the inclusion of most of the poor in large household units with substantial *total* income. If the basis of the distribution is the number of individuals rather than the number of household units, and household income is converted to a per capita basis, then the degree of inequality is comparatively higher. When household size is falling rapidly over time because of changes in the birth rate, this distinction is important. Narrowing differentials in family size imply narrowing differentials in income per household member, the distribution of which would show a greater trend toward equality, or a lesser trend toward inequality, than the commonly calculated distribution of income among households.

In addition to these measurement effects, fertility levels should be expected to influence the transmission of human and physical assets. For example, high-parity children, especially in closely spaced families, tend to receive less care and attention from their parents and often less schooling as well (Leibenstein, 1971; and Wray, 1971). Consequently, they tend to achieve and earn less than low-parity children. Also, high fertility usually implies not only a large number of high-parity children, but also substantial fertility differentials within the population. Differential fertility can be expected to affect income distribution not only because it tends to widen differentials in human capital formation, but also because it tends to widen disparities in the accumulation of material wealth when, as is usually the case, the wealthier have fewer children than the poor (Pryor, 1973). Thus, differences among households in the location of demand and supply curves for human capital tend, as a consequence of varying fertility, to be positively correlated, and the curves themselves are more unequally distributed among households. Both effects increase inequalities in the distribution of income (Becker, 1967).

Fertility levels in the long run are likely to exert macroeconomic effects on distribution. High fertility and rapid population growth will probably be associated with lower wages relative to returns on human and physical capital. Since the ownership of capital is more concentrated by far than the ownership of labor services, higher relative returns to capital with a relatively inelastic factor substitutability would tend to increase the concentration of income. Both macro- and microeconomic mechanisms suggest that higher fertility will lead to inequality in the income distribution (Lindert, 1978).

Specification of the Model. A simple model was constructed for empirical testing on aggregative data. It is intended to capture the crucial interactions between income, its distribution, and demographic processes within the constraints set by the availability of comparable data for a large sample of countries. In this system, fertility, the infant mortality rate, and the distribution of income are all endogenous and mutually inter- acting. For reasons already discussed at length, the fertility rate and the distribution of income within a population must be considered to be determinants of one another. Similarly, the fertility rate and infant mor- tality must be specified to affect each other. It is plausible also to postulate that infant mortality is affected by the distribution of income. However, following the research literature on the subject, in this model the determi- nants of mortality are specified to include female literacy and the nutri- tional situation of the population, two variables which have been found, along with fertility, to be the main influences on child-survival probabili- ties.

The variables which enter into the system are as follows:

Endogenous variables	Exogenous and predetermined variables
Fertility measures	Y, per capita income in 1964
GRR, the gross reproduction	U.S. dollars
rate	FLIT, the female literacy rate
FERT, an approximation to	NEWS, newspaper circulation
the general fertility rate	per thousand population
Mortality measures	DISED, the dispersion of
IMR, the infant mortality rate	adult educational attain
Measures of income distribution	ment
DISTY, the Gini coefficient of	LAND, the share of the small-
income concentration	est 60 percent of holdings
	in total cropped area
	NUTR, average caloric intake
	per capita

Greater detail on the sources and measurements of these data is presented in appendix A.

There are three equations in the system: the first relating the popula- tion fertility rate to average income per capita, its distribution and to in- fant mortality and other variables; the second relating the distribution of income to the fertility level and other variables; and the third explaining the infant mortality rate in terms of fertility and other factors.

In an analogy to the aggregated equation (see Equation 2-3), the current fertility rate is specified to depend both on the average level of income per capita and its distribution. A squared term in income per capita is also called for by the logic of the argument. Discussion of its effects on the estimated equation will be deferred until chapter 6, which deals with international implications. Although its omission from the regression equations reported below would be expected to bias the estimated co-efficients of those variables included—especially that of income per capita —comparison of the results of chapter 2 and chapter 6 reveals that none of the hypothesis tests are substantially altered by this procedure.

It is hypothesized that the more equally income is distributed, the lower the fertility rate of the population. With regard to the influence of average income per capita, no prediction is made. Although the pure income effect on desired family size is expected to be positive, if children are not "inferior goods" in the economic sense, the overall impact of income on actual fertility may be positive or negative in a stock-adjustment process such as that described in appendix B (page 33). The infant mortality rate is expected to be positively related to current fertility through the stock-adjustment mechanism: the higher mortality is, the lower actual family size will be relative to that which is desired. There is considerable evidence for this association (Schultz, 1976). However, since high fertility and closely spaced births also increase infant mortality, a simultaneous interaction is postulated.

The female literacy rate, as a measure of female educational attainment, is hypothesized to be negatively related to fertility, since more widespread literacy is indicative of lower contraceptive costs, a higher opportunity cost of child-rearing, a smaller family size, and a heightened sense of personal efficacy and purposefulness, which should result in placing a higher value on the spacing of births and the achievement of fertility targets. Perhaps in the more advanced countries, where the female literacy rate is very high, it might not be a sensitive indicator of variations in women's educational attainment, but for the mass of the world's population, the literacy rate is still not high. The mean female literacy rate in our sample of countries is only 57 percent. Also, there is evidence from relatively advanced countries that the early years of schooling have a much stronger impact on subsequent fertility than the later years (Ben-

Porath, 1973). However, in some specifications, an alternative measure—newspaper circulation per 1,000 persons—was substituted. This variable is theoretically inferior but more widely available, and it more effectively captures differences in educational levels and access to information in advanced countries, as well as being probably less error-prone than literacy rates obtained through census interviews.

The specification differs from conventional aggregate models of fertility primarily by the inclusion of the population income distribution as an additional influence. This is required by the nonlinearity of the underlying disaggregated process. Omission of this variable leads to bias in the estimates of the remaining coefficients, if the included variables are correlated with the population distribution of income. This implies that past attempts to estimate the effects of infant mortality, or of educational attainment, on fertility from sample observations of countries, regions, or other aggregative data have led to biased estimates because of misspecification, if those variables are associated with the distribution of income and the income distribution strongly affects fertility rates.

With regard to determinants of income distribution, recent theoretical and empirical research has attributed a good deal of the dispersion in earnings to differentials in the stock of human capital within the population, including that acquired through schooling or on-the-job training (Mincer, 1970). In addition, many social scientists point to the underlying structure of a society that influences who will be given educational opportunities and favorable career openings. These structural aspects determine the power and class relationships in a society and are responsible for much of the intergenerational persistence in income levels and inequality.

The basis for the hypothesis that high fertility tends to increase income inequality has already been presented. In addition, the effect of human capital stock distribution is captured by a measure of the dispersion of educational attainment in the adult population. An attempt has been made also to introduce the effect of fundamental structural aspects of the society by a measure of the concentration of agricultural land ownership. This variable has a strict economic interpretation. Since in most of the world's economies agriculture is a major, if not the primary, source of income, and since land is the principal nonlabor input into agriculture, the concentration of land ownership is a measure of the distribution of nonhuman capital. However, beyond this, the concentration of land ownership is also a reasonable indicator of the concentration of political power and influence in most countries, and so probably represents a measure of underlying structural elements in the society. Chapter 5 presents detailed evidence regarding the effect of land concentration on income distribution.

The final variable introduced in the explanation of variations in income distribution is the level of average per capita income. This captures several effects. First, as Chiswick and Mincer (1972) have pointed out, the mean values of the educational stock and the rate of return on capital should be related to the distribution of earnings, and these are systematically related to the level of income. Also, higher income per capita is associated with a lower share of agriculture in total output, and this reduces the seasonality of employment and the variation in hours worked by those in the labor force. Third, higher per capita income is associated with a larger role for government in the economy, and government action is usually redistributive in intent and in effect. It should be noted, however, that many of these tendencies run in opposite directions, and may be partially offsetting.

There is no body of comparable theory on the determinants of infant mortality. There are large numbers of empirical studies, however. A recent survey has identified the factors most closely related to high infant mortality (Russell, 1974). One of these is fertility. High fertility implies high parity and closely spaced births, with a greater proportion of babies born to young or old mothers. The consequences of this are a greater probability of maternal malnourishment, and for the infants, birth complications and abnormalities, low birth weights, and earlier weaning.

In addition to the level of fertility, the average caloric intake per capita was introduced as a measure of the nutritional status of the population. Few cases of protein deficiency are found when there is adequate caloric intake, while protein deficiency is almost always found when caloric intake is found to be deficient, so that the latter is the best single measure of general malnutrition. Malnutrition of the mother during and after pregnancy is associated with low infant birth weights and early weaning, while malnourishment of the child is strongly synergistic with respiratory and intestinal infections and other diseases, substantially raising mortality rates. Finally, the female literacy rate has been used as a measure of mothers' education, which has been found substantially to influence the quality of care given the child, and to have a close association with the infant mortality rate (Sloan, 1971).

The complete model can be written as follows:

$$GRR = f_1 (DISTY, IMR; Y, FLIT)$$

or, alternatively, by using different measures of fertility and educational attainment, as

$$FERT = f_2 (DISTY, IMR; Y, NEWS).$$

The income distribution equation is

$$DISTY = g (FERT; Y, DISED, LAND)$$

and the infant mortality rate is explained by

$$IMR = h (FERT; FLIT, NUTR).$$

By the order conditions on identifiability, there are sufficient predetermined variables excluded from each of the equations to identify the complete system. The female literacy rate and the distribution of land and of educational attainment within the adult population can clearly be taken as predetermined in this context. The level of average income per capita is also a predetermined variable, since it depends on a sequence of past savings and investment decisions which determine the current capital stock, past population growth rates which determine the current labor force, and a largely exogenous flow of productivity changes. Nutritional supply is largely a function of income. These linearized equations were estimated both by single-equation and simultaneous-equation techniques.

The Findings.   The results of ordinary and two-stage least-squares regressions of both fertility measures on income distribution and the other variables are presented in table 2-1. With one exception, over 60 percent of the total variation in fertility is accounted for by the models. All regression coefficients have the expected sign.

There is a consistently close relationship between more equitable income distribution and lower fertility. When the simultaneous influence of fertility on income distribution is taken into account, the effect of distribution on fertility appears larger. In each case, the size of the regression coefficient is larger in the TSLS estimates than in the corresponding OLS regression. From the first regression, in table 2-1, covering the entire sample, a reduction of the Gini coefficient of 0.10 is associated with a gross reproduction rate lower by 0.21. At the sample means of 0.4415 and 2.41, respectively, this implies an elasticity of 0.39. The elasticity, as

Table 2-1. Regressions of Fertility on Income Distribution and Other Variables

Dependent variable	Method	Income distribution	Infant mortality	Female literacy	Income per capita	News circulation	R^2
			Explanatory variables				
Regressions using the entire sample of sixty-eight countries							
GRR	OLS	2.14 (3.46)	.0006 (0.34)	−1.09 (3.21)	−.0004 (3.18)		.69
FERT	OLS	137.3 (4.03)	.140 (2.01)		−.012 (1.32)	−.20 (4.40)	.76
Regressions using the sample of forty-five countries available for simultaneous estimation							
GRR	OLS	3.20 (3.76)	.0029 (1.44)	−1.23 (2.06)	−.0003 (3.07)		.73
GRR	TSLS	7.17 (2.63)	−.0093 (0.63)	−3.02 (1.48)	−.00006 (0.21)		.26
FERT	OLS	184.4 (3.82)	.138 (1.52)		.012 (1.39)	−.19 (3.87)	.78
FERT	TSLS	204.0 (1.43)	.68 (1.63)		.009 (0.73)	−.07 (0.58)	.60

Note: The figures in parentheses are t statistics. See page 23 for an explanation of the variables used in table.

calculated from the regression over the whole sample and using the alternative measure of fertility, is 0.47. Of course, no false precision should be read into these estimates. They are formed from crude, cross-national, cross-sectional data. Also, the Gini coefficient itself is an ambiguous summary statistic of the distribution of income. Yet, they show that the association is a strong one. The increased size of the coefficient, when estimated as part of a wider model, indicates that the association cannot be attributed to the effects of high fertility on the distribution of income, or to the effects on both of other underlying variables encompassed by the model.

Female literacy and the alternative measure of educational attainment are consistently inversely related to fertility. The effects on fertility of increases in average per capita income, *ceteris paribus,* are negative, but small, and often statistically insignificant. The infant mortality rate is positively related to fertility, both in the simple and simultaneous models. From Equation 2-1, the elasticities at the sample means of fertility, with

Table 2-2. Regression of Income Distribution on Fertility and Other Variables

Explanatory variable	Regression coefficient	t statistic
Fertility	0.0007	1.77
Dispersion of education	0.088	1.51
Share of smallest 60 percent of holdings in total area	−0.216	2.22
Average income per capita	−0.154	0.57

Note: R² = 0.45.

respect to the infant mortality rate, average income per capita, and the female adult literacy rate, are 0.02, −0.10, and −0.25, respectively.

Table 2-2 presents the results of the TSLS regression of the Gini coefficient on fertility, as measured by the approximate general fertility rate, income per capita, the dispersion of educational attainment, and the share of the smallest 60 percent of landholdings in total area. All coefficients have the expected sign and, with the exception of average income per capita, are of reasonable size relative to their standard errors. The coefficient of determination is 0.45. No strict probability statements are possible, since tests of significance under this estimation procedure are asymptotically valid, and in this case the sample of forty-five observations is quite small. The estimated elasticity of the Gini coefficient with respect to the fertility rate is .20, which is substantial, but only one-half that of income distribution on fertility. The finding of only a weak association between the level of per capita income and its distribution is not unexpected.

In table 2-3, the TSLS regression of infant mortality on fertility and other variables indicates that high fertility is indeed a substantial factor

Table 2-3. Regression of the Infant Mortality Rate on Fertility and Other Variables

Explanatory variable	Regression coefficient	t statistic
Fertility	0.49	1.25
Female literacy rate	−125.6	3.71
Average caloric intake	0.48	1.42

Note: R^2 = 0.52.

behind high infant mortality, along with nutritional intake and the female literacy rate, the last of which appears to have the closest association with infant mortality. The elasticities of infant mortality with respect to fertility and female literacy are 0.77 and −0.88, respectively. The influence of high fertility on infant mortality seems to be much stronger than the reverse influence, but this is crude evidence on which to base such a conclusion.

Given these interrelationships, it is interesting to consider the total impact of a change in an exogenous variable subject to policy manipulation—the effect of female literacy, for example, on birth, death, and population growth rates. It is clear that the total effect of an increase in female literacy on fertility and infant mortality rates is greater than the direct effects. Illustrative calculations, using the first and last regression equations of table 2-1, suggest that the total effect of a rise in literacy on infant mortality might be 30 percent greater than the direct effect. An analogous calculation indicates that the total effect on fertility would be about 10 percent greater than the direct impact, since the resultant fall in infant mortality would also tend to lower fertility. At the mean of the current sample, represented by a gross reproduction rate of 2.4 and an infant mortality rate of 80 per 1,000, only about one-sixth of the fall in fertility, following a rise in female literacy, would be offset demographically by a fall in infant mortality, so that the impact on the rate of population growth would be substantial.

A similar process of reinforcement results from the positive interaction of fertility and income distribution. As an illustration, using the comparable TSLS regressions in tables 2-1 and 2-2 as a base, the total effects of a redistribution of landholdings on income distribution is 20 percent larger than the direct effect, because of the positive feedback from fertility. At the same time, each increase of ten percentage points in the share of the smallest 60 percent of holdings in the total agricultural area is estimated to reduce fertility by about 5 percent.

The evidence from aggregative data, therefore, is strongly supportive of the hypothesized association between income concentration and high fertility. For any level of average income, greater inequality in its distribution is associated with a higher population fertility rate. This is consistent with the underlying nonlinear effect of income on current fertility at the household level. Chapters 3 and 4 explore this disaggregative process directly.

APPENDIX A: THE DATA

Two measures of fertility have been used. One consists of the annual number of births divided by one-half the population aged fifteen to sixty-four. It is an approximation to the general fertility rate, which is usually defined as the annual number of births divided by the number of women in the age group fifteen to forty-four. This variable, available from 112 countries for years in the mid-1960s, was computed from data from Harbison, Maruhnic, and Resnick (1970).

An alternative, widely used measure of fertility is the gross reproduction rate, a period rate measuring the number of daughters a woman would have if she lived through her reproductive period manifesting the same age-specific fertility rates as the current population of women. This measure was available from the UN (1974) for all the countries of the sample. These data refer to the period 1965–70, a somewhat later period than that for the other data, most of which refer to the period 1960–65. Consequently, this variable is less suitable as an explanatory variable in regressions of the distribution of income and the infant mortality rate. It is perhaps more suitable for use in ordinary least-squares regressions in which fertility is the dependent variable, since the implicit lag should reduce the degree of simultaneity between the dependent variable and the regressors.

In earlier research on this topic, two measures of income distribution were used: the share of total personal income received by the poorest 40 percent of the population, and the Gini coefficient (King and coauthors, 1974). It was found that these two measures were correlated to the extent of 0.95 across the sample, and gave very similar results in the analysis. Consequently, only one measure, the Gini coefficient, which is somewhat more general, has been used (Jain and Tiemann, 1973). Since the number of countries for which data on income distribution are available limits the overall size of the sample, additional effort has been made to gather more data, yielding distribution data for a half-dozen more countries.[1]

The primary source of data on the infant mortality and female literacy rates was the UN (1974), but other sources were used to fill in missing observations for a number of countries.[2] Data on average daily caloric intake

[1] The sources for this additional data are as follows: Australia (Podder, 1972); Bolivia, Morocco, Nigeria, Surinam, Trinidad, and Tobago (Adelman and Morris, 1971); and Ghana (Ewasi, 1971).

[2] Other general sources included Taylor and Hudson (1972); for Korea, Cho (1973); for Iran, Population Council (1972); and for Ghana, Population Council (1970).

For certain advanced countries in which literacy rates are quite high, including Australia, Canada, Czechoslovakia, Denmark, the Federal Republic of

were obtained from Harbison, Maruhnic, and Resnick (1970), along with per capita income figures (on GNP at factor cost expressed in U.S. dollars at 1964 prices).

Data on the distribution of landholdings were obtained from the UN (FAO, 1971). The concept of holding refers to use rather than ownership, and holdings are undoubtedly more equally distributed than ownership because of the widespread practices of renting and sharecropping. Data were available on the percentage of total agricultural area and the percentage of total holdings by size of holdings. From these were estimated the share of the total area held by the smallest 40, 50, and 60 percent of holders. These are highly correlated, and only the last was subsequently used in the analysis. Apart from the distinction between landowners and landholders, there are other deficiencies in the variable. Holdings under 1 acre were excluded from the figures. For many countries, especially in Asia, a very substantial fraction of all holdings are thus excluded. Also, no distinction is made in the data between different kinds of agricultural land, that is, between irrigated versus unirrigated, or cropland versus grazing land. Consequently, this variable can be taken only as a very approximate measure of the concentration of land ownership, subject to substantial measurement error.

A crude measure of the dispersion of the educational attainment of the adult population was also the best that could be calculated from available data. The UNESCO *Statistical Yearbook,* for various years since 1965, presents information on the proportions of the adult population (twenty-five years old and older, with some exceptions) who have less than a primary school education, and who have completed primary, secondary, and tertiary education. There are some differences among countries in the number of school years included in each level; and, in addition, the year of reference varies from country to country, mostly within the period 1960–65. Some missing observations were filled in with data from Dennison (1967). The measure of dispersion was formed by weighting the percentages in each educational category by the number of categories separating it from the modal category, which thus received a zero weight. For example, in Algeria the percentages in each category were 91.8, 6.0, 1.8, and 0.4, respectively, so that the measure of dispersion was $1 \times 6.0 + 2 \times 1.8 + 3 \times 0.4 = 10.8$.

The sample used for estimation of the complete model was limited in size by the availability of data on the dispersion of the educational stock and

---

Germany, Finland, the Netherlands, Norway, Sweden, and the United States, the female adult illiteracy rates were estimated by the percentage of adult women with no schooling. For lack of alternative sources, the same method was used for Ghana, Guyana, Kenya, South Africa, Trinidad, and Tobago. Adult schooling rates were taken from UNESCO's *Statistical Yearbooks*. Other country data sources were, for Burma, (UNESCO, 1972, tab. 14); and, for Taiwan (Population Council, 1970).

of landholdings. Forty-five observations were available for this purpose, whereas sixty-eight country data points could be used to estimate the fertility equation alone by ordinary least squares.

APPENDIX B: A STOCK-ADJUSTMENT MODEL OF CURRENT FERTILITY

The model of current marital fertility presented in this appendix is intended only to illustrate the diverse ways in which household income may affect household fertility when the latter is subject to imperfect and costly control, and to show how nonlinearities are likely to arise in the influence of income on fertility. Only those aspects of the model are featured; other implications are not fully developed.

At a particular age t an individual married woman could be assumed to have, if there were no costs to fertility control, a desired family size N_t^*. This number can be regarded as a demand jointly determined with the demands for other goods and services, and with the allocation of the time of household members through a process of constrained welfare maximization. Welfare maximization models of this type, constrained by the wealth and time resources of the household, have been presented by many economists (Becker, 1960; Rosenzweig and Evenson, 1976; and Willis, 1973) and need not be reconstructed here. The demand for children in such a process depends upon household wealth, the price of children, and the price of close substitutes, usually assumed to be children of greater resource intensity (that is, of higher quality).

The price of children is determined largely by the opportunity costs of the mother's time and by the infant mortality rate. The price of more resource-intensive children depends mainly on the direct and opportunity costs of schooling, which include the forgone rewards to child labor attributable to school attendance. Therefore,

$$N_t^* = N^*(Y_t, p_{nt}, p_{st}, T) \tag{B-1}$$

where Y represents household nonlabor income; T represents the total time resources of the household; p_n represents a vector of variables outside the range of household control determining the price of a child; and p_s another set of exogenous factors determining the total price of schooling and other investments in the child's well-being.

Current fertility is a random variable, however. The natural fertility of a woman P_t, measured in terms of the probability of conception within a given time interval, can be modified through application of some technique of birth control with a contraceptive efficiency e. Associated with each contraceptive efficiency e, there is a certain minimum cost, including both psychic and material disadvantages. These costs can be represented by a schedule in which average and marginal costs are near zero for no birth control and rise rapidly as efficiency approaches unity:

$$C(e) = ae^2 \qquad 0 \le e < 1 \tag{B-2}$$

The benefits from birth control are derived from the welfare losses of departures from the ideal family size (Michael and Willis, 1976), augmented by the advantages of child spacing. The first can be described by a function which rises rapidly as actual family size exceeds the ideal, and falls as the actual family size falls short of the ideal. The second can be represented by a function which rises with the probability of conceiving in the current period. These components are multiplicative. The desirability of wide spacing is lower, the further actual family size is beneath the ideal; the desirability of wide spacing is higher, the more the actual exceeds the ideal. Thus, a suitable cost function from which the benefits of fertility control can be derived is shown in Equation B:

$$B(e) = A - m[P(1 - e)]^2(k) / exp[r(N^* - N)] \tag{B-3}$$

The parameters have clear-cut interpretations, as is illustrated in figure B-1. When actual family size equals the ideal, k is the welfare cost of an additional child, apart from spacing considerations. The parameter r determines the pace at which these welfare costs change from deviations from the ideal, while A is simply a scalar which transforms costs to benefits at some small family size below the ideal. The spacing parameter m measures essentially the welfare

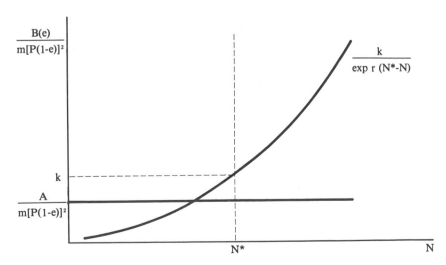

Figure B-1. The benefits of birth control as a function of desired and actual family size.

costs of a higher probability of conception within the current period. This cost is conditioned by the woman's position of excess or deficit fertility.

Clearly, the welfare-maximizing household will minimize the sum of the welfare costs of contraception and the welfare costs of excessive and too rapid fertility. This implies setting the marginal costs of contraception equal to the marginal costs of childbearing, where both are expressed in terms of the probabilities of conceiving. This condition amounts to the stipulation that for the optimal degree of fertility control e^*,

$$ae^* = kmP(1 - e^*)/exp\,[r\,(N^* - N)]\qquad\qquad\text{(B-4)}$$

It is helpful to define a new parameter b as the ratio of costs to benefits from a marginal change in contraceptive efficiency at the ideal family size.

$$b = a/kmP\qquad\qquad\text{(B-5)}$$

Then,

$$(1 - e^*)/e^* = bexp\,[r\,(N^* - N)]\qquad\qquad\text{(B-6)}$$

And,

$$e^* = \frac{1}{1 + bexp\,[r\,(N^* - N)]}\qquad\qquad\text{(B-7)}$$

A woman with N children who desires N^* would choose a contraceptive technique with efficiency e^*. The behavior of e^* is depicted in figure B-2. Birth

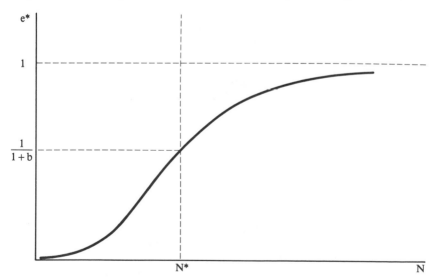

Figure B-2. The optimal degree of fertility control as a function of actual and desired family size.

control would be near zero at family sizes well below the ideal, and rise to nearly complete efficiency as family size exceeds that desired. Typically, a woman with the ideal number of children would not optimally use contraception with perfect efficiency unless the marginal cost of contraception were zero. Consequently, the expected completed family size would be greater than that which would be ideal with costless fertility control.

The optimal degree of fertility control is related in predictable ways to the underlying parameters of the model. It will be higher, the higher the natural fertility of the woman, the lower the marginal costs of contraception, and the higher the welfare costs of excess fertility and close birth spacing. Other things being equal, it will be higher, the higher the actual stock of children is relative to that number currently desired.

This optimal degree of contraception gives rise to a conditional birth probability for the individual woman in each time period:

$$P_t^* = P^*(\Delta N / \Delta t / N_t^*, N_t, b, r) = P_t (1 - e_t^*).$$ (B-8)

This, aside from gestation lags, is her fertility rate for the current period. To complete the process, expected family size in any interval is generated by the following recursive process:

$$E(N_{t+1}) = N_t (1 - w_t) + P^* \qquad N_0 = 0$$ (B-9)

where w_t is the expected infant mortality rate applicable to the household in the period t.

The conditional birth probability P^* represents a simple stock-adjustment process; that is, the greater the existing stock of children, the lower the current fertility rate. Within this framework, the diverse influences of income can be distinguished. Income might be expected to influence not only ideal family size, but also, through the infant mortality rate, the existing stock of children. The influence of income might also extend to the perceived costs of departures from ideal family size, and to the desirability attached to child spacing. Finally, the economic status of the household could influence the natural fertility of the woman and the perceived costs of fertility control. It is clear that whatever restrictions there are on the sign of $\partial N^*/\partial Y$ through the formation of consumer demands, there are no restrictions on the sign of $\partial P^*/\partial Y$. Moreover, under only the remotest of circumstances could P^* be represented as a linear function of Y. In general, $\partial P^*/\partial Y$ will be a complicated function of Y itself. The quadratic expression employed in the text, in Equation B-1, and in the subsequent empirical investigations can be regarded as a second-order approximation to a more complex relation such as the one just derived.

REFERENCES

Adelman, I., and C. T. Morris. 1971. *An Anatomy of Patterns of Income Distribution in Developing Nations,* Final Report, AID grant csd-226 (Evanston, Ill., Northwestern University Press).

Askham, Janet. 1975. *Fertility and Deprivation* (Cambridge, England, Cambridge University Press).

Becker, Gary. 1960. "An Economic Analysis of Fertility," in *Demographic and Economic Change in Developed Countries,* Universities-National Bureau Conferences Series, No. 11 (Princeton, N.J., Princeton University Press).

———. 1967. *Human Capital and the Size Distribution of Income: An Analytical Approach,* W. S. Woytinsky Lecture No. 1 (Ann Arbor, Institute of Public Administration, University of Michigan).

———. 1973. "A Theory of Marriage: Part I," *Journal of Political Economy* vol. 81, no. 4 (July/August) pp. 813–846.

———. 1974. "A Theory of Marriage: Part II," *Journal of Political Economy* vol. 82, no. 2 (March/April) pp. 11–26.

Ben-Porath, Yoram. 1973. "Fertility in Israel: Point and Counterpoint," *Journal of Political Economy* vol. 81, no. 2, pt. 2 (suppl. March/April) pp. 202–233.

Bernhardt, E. 1972. "Fertility and Economic Status: Some Recent Findings on Differentials in Sweden," *Population Studies* vol. 26, no. 2 (July) pp. 175–206.

Chiswick, Barry, and Jacob Mincer. 1972. "Time Series Changes in Personal Income Inequality in the U.S. from 1939, with Projections to 1985," in "Investment in Education: The Equity-Efficiency Quandary," *Journal of Political Economy* vol. 80, no. 3, pt. 2 (suppl. May/June) pp. 34–66.

Cho, L. J. 1973. "The Demographic Situation in the Republic of Korea," in *Papers of the East-West Population Institute,* no. 29 (Honolulu, Hawaii, East–West Center).

Dennison, Edward. 1967. *Why Growth Rates Differ* (Paris, OECD).

Easterlin, R. A. 1975. "An Economic Framework for Fertility Analysis," *Studies in Family Planning* vol. 6, no. 3 (March 1975) pp. 24–36.

Ewasi, K. 1971. "Notes on the Relative Distribution of Income in Developing Countries," *Review of Income and Wealth* ser. 17, no. 4 (December) pp. 371–375.

Frisch, Rose. 1974. *Demographic Implications of the Biological Determinants of Female Fecundity,* Research Papers Series (Cambridge, Mass., Center for Population Studies, Harvard University).

Gregory, Paul R., and J. M. Campbell, Jr. 1976. "Fertility Interactions and

Modernization Turning Points," *Journal of Political Economy* vol. 84, no. 4, pt. I (August) pp. 835–849.

Harbison, Frederick H., Joan Maruhnic, and Jane R. Resnick. 1970. *Quantitative Aspects of Modernization and Development.* Research Report No. 115, Princeton University, Department of Economics, Industrial Relations Section (Princeton, N.J., Princeton University Press).

Hashimoto, Masanori. 1974. "Economics of Postwar Fertility in Japan; Differentials and Trends," *Journal of Political Economy* vol. 82, no. 2, pt. 2 (suppl. March/April) pp. 170–194.

Hout, Michael. 1977. "Economic and Sociological Explanations of Marital Fertility in the United States, 1967–1970." Paper presented to the annual meeting of the Population Association of America, Saint Louis, Missouri (April).

Huffman, Sandra, J. Chakraborty, and W. Henry Moseley. 1977. "Nutrition and Postpartum Amenorrhea in Rural Bangladesh." Paper presented to the annual meeting of the Population Association of America, Saint Louis, Missouri (April).

Inkeles, A., and David Smith. 1974. *Becoming Modern: Individual Change in Six Developing Countries* (Cambridge, Mass., Harvard University Press).

Jain, S., and A. Tiemann. 1973. "Size Distribution of Income: Compilation of Data," International Bank for Reconstruction and Development, Development Research Center, Discussion Paper No. 4 (Washington, D.C., IBRD).

King, Timothy, Robert Cuca, Ravi Gulhati, Monowar Hossain, Ernest Stern, Pravin Visaria, K. C. Zachariah, Gregory Zafros, B. Meredith Burke, Bonnie Newlon, and Robert Repetto. 1974. *Population Policies and Economic Development: The World Bank Staff Report* (Washington, D.C., World Bank).

Kocher, James E. 1974. *Rural Development, Equity, and Fertility Decline* (New York, Population Council).

Kuznets, Simon. 1975. "Demographic Components in the Size Distribution of Income," (New Haven, Conn., Economic Growth Center, Yale University) Mimeo.

Lee, Ronald D. 1977. "Target Fertility, Contraception, and Aggregate Rates: Toward a Formal Synthesis" (Ann Arbor, Population Studies Center, University of Michigan) Mimeo.

Leibenstein, Harvey. 1971. "The Impact of Population Growth on Economic Welfare: Non-traditional Elements," in *Rapid Population Growth.* Prepared by a Study Committee of the Office of the Foreign Secretary, National Academy of Sciences, with the support of the Agency for International Development (Baltimore, Md., The Johns Hopkins University Press).

Lindert, Peter. 1978. *Fertility and Scarcity in America* (Princeton, N.J., Princeton University Press).

Michael, Robert T., and Robert J. Willis. 1976. "Contraception and Fertility: Household Production under Uncertainty," in Nester E. Terleckyj, ed., *Household Production and Consumption,* Studies in Income and Wealth, vol. 40, by the Conference on Research in Income and Wealth (New York, Columbia University Press for the National Bureau of Economic Research).

Mincer, Jacob. 1970. "The Distribution of Labor Incomes: A Survey with Special Reference to the Human Capital Approach," *Journal of Economic Literature* vol. 8, no. 1 (March) pp. 1–26.

Paglin, Morton. 1975. "The Measurement and Trend of Inequality: A Basic Revision," *American Economic Review* vol. 65, no. 3 (September) pp. 598–609.

Podder, N. 1972. "Distribution of Household Income in Australia," *Economic Record* vol. 48, no. 122 (June) pp. 181–200.

Population Council. 1970. *Country Profiles: Ghana* (New York, Population Council).

———. 1972. *Country Profiles: Iran* (New York, Population Council).

Pryor, Frederick. 1973. "Simulation of the Impact of Social and Economic Institutions on the Size Distribution of Income and Wealth," *American Economic Review* vol. 63, no. 1 (March) pp. 50–72.

Rich, William. 1973. *Smaller Families Through Social and Economic Progress* (Washington, D.C., Overseas Development Council).

Rosenzweig, M. R., and R. Evenson. 1976. "Fertility, Schooling and the Economic Contribution of Children in Rural India." Paper presented at the annual meeting of the Population Association of America, Montreal (April).

Russell, Louise. 1974. *Determinants of Infant and Child Mortality: Report of Feasibility Study* (Washington, D.C., National Planning Association).

Ryder, Norman. 1973. "Comment," *Journal of Political Economy* vol. 81, no. 2, pt. 2 (suppl., March/April) pp. 65–69.

Sanderson, W., and R. Willis. 1971. "Economic Models of Fertility: Some Examples and Implications," *Annual Report* (Washington, D.C., National Bureau of Economic Research).

Schultz, T. Paul. 1974. *Fertility Determinants: A Theory, Evidence and an Application to Policy Evaluation* (Santa Monica, Calif., Rand Corporation) pp. 2–6.

———. 1976. "Fertility and Mortality," in Ronald Ridker, ed., *Population and Development: The Search for Selective Interventions* (Baltimore, Md., Johns Hopkins University Press for Resources for the Future).

———. 1977. "An Economic Interpretation of the Decline in Fertility in a Rapidly Developing Country: Consequences of Development and Family

Planning," Discussion Paper (New Haven, Conn., Yale University, Economic Growth Center).

Simon, Julian. 1974. *The Effects of Income on Fertility,* Monograph 19, (Chapel Hill, N.C., Carolina Population Center).

Sloan, F. 1971. *Survival of Progeny in Developing Countries* (Santa Monica, Calif., Rand Corporation).

Snyder, Don. 1975. "An Econometric Analysis of the Decision to Have Additional Children." Paper presented to the Third Congress of the Econometric Society, Toronto (August).

Taylor, C. L., and M. C. Hudson. 1972. *World Handbook of Political and Social Indicators* (New Haven, Conn., Yale University Press and the Population Reference Bureau).

Tobin, James. 1973. "Comments," *Journal of Political Economy* vol. 81, no. 2 pt. 2 (suppl., March/April) pp. S275–S278.

Thornton, Arland, and Joo Chul Kim. 1977. "Perceived Impact of Financial Considerations on Childbearing." Paper presented to the annual meeting of the Population Association of America, Saint Louis, Mo. (April).

Turchi, Boone. 1975. *The Demand for Children* (Cambridge, Mass., Ballinger).

United Nations. *Demographic Yearbooks* (various years).

United Nations. 1963. *Population Bulletin No. 7* (New York, UN).

United Nations, Department of Economic and Social Affairs, Statistical Office. 1974. Statistical Papers, series A, vol. XXVI, no. 1, *Population and Vital Statistics Report* (New York, UN).

United Nations, Food and Agriculture Organization. 1971. *Report on the 1960 World Census of Agriculture,* vol. 5 (Rome, FAO).

UNESCO. *Statistical Yearbook* (various years since 1965).

———. 1972. *Progress of Education in the Asian Region* (Bangkok, UNESCO).

Wilkinson, Maurice. 1973. "An Econometric Analysis of Fertility in Sweden, 1870–1965," *Econometrica* vol. 41, no. 4 (July) pp. 633–642.

Willis, Robert. 1973. "A New Approach to the Economic Theory of Fertility Behavior," *Journal of Political Economy* vol. 81, no. 2, pt. 2 (suppl. March/April) pp. S14–S64.

Wray, Joe D. 1971. "Population Pressure on Families: Family Size and Child Spacing," *Reports on Population/Family Planning* no. 9, (August).

3 ⌐⌐ EVIDENCE FROM PUERTO RICAN HOUSEHOLD DATA

This chapter presents the results of an investigation into the effect of income distribution on fertility and is based on demographic and economic information pertaining to individual households. The approach thus circumvents the problems associated with the analysis of aggregative data by drawing on information on households within the same community. The foundation of this approach is the investigation of nonlinearities in the relationship between income and fertility, because only if the relationship between household income and fertility were linear would the distribution of income among households be irrelevant to the aggregated fertility rate of the entire population.

Puerto Rico was selected as the focus for this phase of the study for a variety of reasons, some of which are extremely practical. It is a developing region undergoing rapid structural, social, and economic change. Demographic change has been equally rapid. At the same time, the quality of the data base is unusually high for a developing area, and access to it is easy. It was possible to secure for the Puerto Rican population a large-scale representative sample of households, with relatively reliable information for all households on both demographic and economic variables. It is rare to encounter a data source which fulfills all of these conditions simultaneously. Moreover, the data contained information not only on the individual households, but also on the communities in which they live, facilitating the testing of hypotheses concerning the effects of community characteristics on individual household behavior.

The data source used was the 1 percent Public Use Sample for Puerto Rico of the 1970 U.S. Census of Population. This yielded information on approximately 6,850 women of reproductive age, residing in

41

approximately 6,300 households. The households were located in 615 neighborhood units for which information was also available. The data thus consist of a cross-sectional sample of women living in urban and rural areas under different socioeconomic conditions. Inferences made from these data about the changes which might ensue, should economic changes affect individual households *over time,* encounter the usual pitfalls attendant on the use of cross-sectional information. See table 3-1 for a glossary of the variables used in the statistical analysis, including their definitions, acronyms, means, and standard deviations.

In summary, the evidence indicates that a more equal distribution of income would tend to be associated with a lower overall fertility rate. There is a substantial difference in the response of fertility to income changes between high- and low-income households. The results give considerable support to the hypothesis that fertility in Puerto Rico is a stock-adjustment process. Other things equal, there is a substantial inverse relationship between the stock of children living in the family, and the probability of a current birth.

THE PUERTO RICAN BACKGROUND

Puerto Rico's history as a slave colony of Spain and a colonial dependency of the United States for a period of more than four hundred years created as its heritage a specialized and tardy development, based on absentee-owned, large-scale production for export; the absence of an indigenous middle class of small proprietors in agriculture, industry, and finance; an early proletarianization of the labor force; pronounced inequalities in wealth and class divisions within the society; and stunted traditions of civic responsibility.

In 1898, at the end of Spanish rule, all the island could carry forward as its legacy was a literacy rate of about 23 percent, a school-enrollment rate of 8 percent, a capital city with a population of 35,000, a cultivable area with 79 percent of the land lying unused, no banks, two or three roads, and only 20 km of railroad track (Lewis, 1963, page 55). During the next forty years, American rule brought massive economic penetration and the rapid conversion of the island into an agricultural factory for the large-scale production of sugar. Although there were larger expenditures on education, health, and infrastructure during this period, all hopes for the emergence of an indigenous capitalism out of small and medium-sized farms, local industries, and commercial ventures were fore-

Table 3-1. Glossary of Variables Used in the Various Statistical Analyses

Variable acronym	Mean	Standard derivation	Variable description
CEB	2.09	2.67	Children ever born alive to women aged 15 and older
CLT 2	0.16	0.42	The number of own children alive in the household <2 years old, per mother
AGEWMSQ	900.5	627.5	Square of age of women 15 years and older
AGEWM	28.2	10.3	Age of women 15 years and older
HHYCAP	10.8	13.0	Total household income per household member in 1969, in hundreds of dollars
HHYCAPSQ	287.6	1066	Square of household income per member
NEDUC	8.3	2.87	Medium years of schooling completed by population fifteen years and older, in the neighborhood of the respondent household
NFERT	4.2	1.31	Mean children ever born per woman aged 35 to 44 in the neighborhood of respondent
NGINE	.455	.067	The Gini coefficient of concentration of household income in the neighborhood of respondent
LEGMAR	0.56	0.49	A dummy variable, 1 if the woman is legally married currently, zero otherwise
CONMAR	0.04	0.21	A dummy variable, if the woman, 15 years or older, is consensually married, zero otherwise
WRKD3Y	0.35	0.48	A dummy variable, 1 if the woman is currently employed or has worked in previous 3 years
EDUCWM	10.6	4.48	Years of schooling completed by woman
ENRATE	.87	.17	Fraction of own children aged 6 to 16 currently enrolled in school
VARYHD	396	196	The sum of sample variances of income of men in same occupation, sector, and employment category as spouse of woman
CEB2PLUS	1.92	2.62	The number of own children of woman 2 years old or older

stalled by the inrush of mainland corporate enterprise in trade, finance, transport, and, particularly, in sugar production. During the late 1920s and the 1930s, medium-scale Puerto Rican sugar producers were forced by market pressures to sell their holdings to big integrated producers, whose large-scale organizations could continue to profit when the smaller producer could not. At the same time, crops such as tobacco and tropical products, as well as food crops for local consumption, suffered since almost exclusive attention and investment went toward the sugar economy. During this period a large rural proletariat was created, as well as a rapidly expanding but impoverished migrant population in San Juan and other cities.

It was only at the time of the New Deal and the rise to power of Luis Munoz Marin that substantial changes could be recorded in what Lewis (1966) terms "the imperialism of neglect." The attention of New Deal liberals like Rexford Tugwell and Harold Ickes, as well as the leadership of the first Puerto Rican politician with a mass following, reversed the practice of "negative government" that has been typical of all colonial administrations. The creation of administrative machinery for positive action, the formulation of ambitious development programs like that of the Puerto Rican Land Authority, which managed, at least, to make a start at the redistribution of land held by the large sugar corporations, and the inflow of substantial development funds from the U.S. government improved living conditions on the island and broadened the base of the physical and educational infrastructure. Perhaps even more important, it created a momentum of planning and expectations for further development which, although abruptly interrupted by World War II, would be resumed in the postwar period.

During the postwar period, economic growth in Puerto Rico was rapid by any standards. Between 1940 and 1960, the real GNP rose by an annual average rate of 5.8 percent. At the heart of this growth rate was industrialization, spurred by liberal tax incentives and other inducements, as well as ready supplies of low-wage labor. A large number of U.S. firms set up branch plants in Puerto Rico for export of goods back to the mainland, often as convenient and lucrative tax shelters. Perhaps equally important was the inflow of capital, not only in the form of large federal transfers under a wide variety of programs, but also through the marketing of a wide variety of Puerto Rican capital liabilities (Ingram, 1962). Structural change during this period was remarkable. The share of employment in agriculture fell from 35 percent to 17 percent, employment in home industries and domestic services gave place to factory and commercial employment, and the dominating role of sugar in the economy was diminished.

Labor-force movements were dramatic (Reynolds and Gregory, 1965). During the 1940s the labor-force participation rate of women aged twenty and older rose substantially, while in the ensuing decade the rise in the participation rate in the modern sector was offset by an equally dramatic fall in employment in the home needlework industries and other traditional sources of employment for women such as agriculture and domestic service. During the 1950s there was massive out-migration from Puerto Rico to the mainland, to the extent that during this entire decade the Puerto Rican labor force scarcely grew. At its end, 27 percent of all Puerto Ricans lived on the mainland, most of them in and around New York City. The importance of this emigration to the development of Puerto Rico can scarcely be overestimated.

The motivating factors were clear. Despite the rapid economic growth on the island, unemployment remained high, and wage levels, although rising, remained substantially lower than those prevailing in comparable industries on the mainland. Puerto Ricans endured the cultural dislocation and considerable indignities of life on the mainland for the sake of the economic gains, which, on the average, amounted to earnings two or three times those of island workers. Migration was extremely selective of young adults having seven or eight years of education. Among older Puerto Ricans there was a substantial return flow of migration so that, in 1960, fully 5 percent of the people on the island were returning migrants (Sandis, 1970. page 2).

Partly as a consequence of this massive outflow of labor, and also as the result of minimum-wage legislation, which effectively pushed up wage levels both in the industrial sector and in traditional sectors not covered by regulation, skill differentials narrowed in the Puerto Rican wage structure. Puerto Rican wage levels, as a whole, rose from a quarter of the U.S. mainland level in 1950 to nearly one-half that in 1963 (Reynolds and Gregory, 1965). One consequence of this was an increase in the capital intensity of industrial production and a considerable rationalization of labor utilization.

Throughout this period of dramatic economic change, what published evidence there is seems to indicate that there was no substantial change in the overall distribution of income. According to an estimate published by Weisskopf for 1953 and 1963, the Gini index rose mildly from .42 to .45, but other indexes showed growing equality over the period (Weisskopf, 1970). According to these data, the share of the middle-income groups grew at the expense of both the top and the bottom. This is indeed surprising in view of the wage movements, the emigration, the liberal fiscal treatment of profits, the greatly increased flow of transfer payments, and public welfare expenditures—all of which might have been expected to produce something other than a continuation of the status quo.

However, there was a distinct change in the social environment of Puerto Rico over this period, and also in family relationships. The cultural starting point within the household was an authoritarian family structure with markedly differentiated sex roles, involving social and economic dependency for women, aggressive and exploitative postures for men, and extremely precarious marital communication and adjustment (Stycos, 1955). Considerable research has shown that along with the rising educational levels of women and their greatly increased participation in modern industrial and commercial employment has come a greater degree of autonomy for them, and a shift in family relations toward greater equality and balance in communication and decision-making (Joseph, 1967).

In the social realm, the preindustrial order entailed considerable social stratification based on wealth, color, and occupation. The rapid economic growth and change of the past generation has brought about a large amount of intra- and intergenerational mobility (Tumin and Feldman, 1961). It has also brought about a widespread diffusion of perceived American values, including the creation of a competitive status-ranking system based on the acquisition, use, and display of prestige-bearing consumption items, which has allowed the nouveau riche within a generation to assert their claims to upper-class social standing. According to Tumin and Feldman (1961), it has also brought along with it a great deal of anxiety and frustration for middle-class households who constantly are faced with the temptation to measure their life-style and possessions of the moment against those of households just above or below them on the social ladder.

It would be surprising if along with this economic and social transformation, there had not been a demographic transformation as well. The demographic changes which have taken place since 1950 have been dramatic. The crude birth rate, which was around 40 per 1,000 in the period 1945–50, had fallen to around 25 per 1,000 by 1970. The growth rate of population, which had peaked in the years immediately after World War II, had fallen to around 2 percent per annum by the end of the 1960s. Tables 3-2 through 3-5 give the main elements of the Puerto Rican vital statistics in historical perspective and show the more recent history of fertility declines in greater detail.

Table 3-2. The Demographic Evolution of Puerto Rico, 1899–1960

Years	Crude birth rate	Crude death rate	Size of population (in thousands)	Yearly rate of natural increase (%)
1900–10	40.5	25.3	963	1.5
1910–20	40.4	24.0	1,117	1.6
1920–30	39.3	22.1	1,299	1.7
1930–40	39.6	19.6	1,544	2.0
1940–45	40.6	15.7	1,869	2.5
1945–50	41.6	12.4	2,210	2.9
1950–60	35.0	6.9	2,360	2.7

Source: Lloyd G. Reynolds and Peter Gregory, *Wages, Productivity and Industrialization in Puerto Rico* (New Haven, Conn., Yale University Press, 1965) p. 29.

Table 3-2 conveys the impression of a region pulling itself back from the brink of demographic disaster. Puerto Rico, faced with the prospect of a demographic explosion after the radical fall in mortality following World War II, never found itself subjected to rates of population growth of 3 percent per year, as have so many of its Latin American neighbors. A combination of fertility decline and emigration kept the population increase in bounds. In fact, as has been pointed out by Davis (1973, page v), the total increase in the Puerto Rican population over the period 1940–70 has been, in percentage terms, *smaller* than that of the mainland.

Vasquez (1968) has demonstrated that, even prior to World War II, the apparent stability in the birth rate masked changes. Nuptiality rose during the first half of the century, and was offset by slow but consistent declines in marital fertility. Indeed, declines in marital fertility have dominated in the demographic transition of Puerto Rico. Changes in age and marital structure of the population have been very important only during the decade of the 1950s, the period of massive out-migration (Vasquez, 1968).

Table 3-3 presents estimates of age-specific fertility rates for 1950, 1960, 1965, and 1970. This information indicates that accelerating fertility declines affect all age groups as time goes on within this interval. Over the twenty-year period, the total fertility rate had fallen from 5.2 to 3.2, a decline of 38 percent. Presser (1973) has shown that female sterilization played a very important role in bringing about this rapid decline. Faced, at least until recently, with poor marital communications and lack of access to more suitable contraceptive methods, Puerto Ricans in large

Table 3-3.   Recent Declines in Puerto Rican Age-Specific Fertility Rates

Period	Age of mother							Total fertility rate
	15–19	20–24	25–29	30–34	35–39	40–44	45–49	
1950	99.2	279.7	260.5	199.5	142.6	52.7	11.5	5.2
1960	96.4	278.8	234.1	154.3	107.1	50.1	9.0	4.6
Change, 1950–60	−2.8	−1.0	−26.4	−45.2	−35.5	−2.6	−2.5	−0.6
1965	92.0	244.7	210.9	132.4	92.6	33.6	7.8	4.0
Change, 1960–65	−4.4	−34.1	−23.2	−21.9	−14.5	−16.6	−1.2	−0.6
1970	75.1	187.7	179.4	105.6	61.7	19.9	3.1	3.2
Change, 1965–70	−16.9	−57.0	−31.5	−26.8	−30.9	−13.7	−4.7	−0.8

Source: Harriet Presser, *Sterilization and Fertility Decline in Puerto Rico*, Population Monograph Series, no. 13 (Berkeley, University of California Press, 1973) pp. 84–91.

numbers have undergone sterilization. By 1965 one-third of all married women had been sterilized. Data indicate a trend toward sterilization at younger ages and lower parities, especially among middle-class women, whose sterilization rates are higher and who seem to have been using the operation as a drastic means of enforcing their fertility goals. By contrast, lower-class women who have lower rates of sterilization, tend to undergo the operation at higher parities and after a history of contraceptive failure. Table 3-4 presents data from the Presser study.

The pronounced curvilinearity in the relationship between the percentage of women sterilized and income, with or without controls on parity, is noteworthy, since it virtually mirrors the curvilinear relationship which will be shown to exist between income and fertility.

For contemporary Puerto Rico, the stock-adjustment model of fertility determination, presented in chapter two, seems to apply. Only supply considerations seem irrelevant to the process. With an average per capita income of over $1,000 per year, Puerto Rico has probably reached a level of economic development over the past generation at which few women exist in such poverty or circumstances that fecundity is impaired. Also, infant mortality rates have fallen to about 28 per 1,000, and at these levels they are probably not an important influence on fertility, even though the remaining infant mortality is differentially distributed among socioeconomic strata.

Table 3-4. Percentage Sterilized of All Mothers Aged Twenty to Forty in 1965, by Family Income and Total Births

Total births	Family income (in U.S.$)				
	<$1,000	$1,000–2,000	$2,000–3,000	$3,000–5,000	Over $5,000
1–2	24.1	32.4	28.9	43.8	18.1
3–4	32.7	44.4	56.2	49.0	47.3
>5	15.4	28.8	28.4	46.3	40.9
Total %	21.2	35.1	38.0	45.8	32.2

Source: Harriet Presser, *Sterilization and Fertility Decline in Puerto Rico*, Population Monograph Series, no. 13 (Berkeley, University of California Press, 1973) p. 135.

There seems to have been a convergence over the past generation in family-size norms and in the factors underlying the demand for children. There is still an inverse association between stated family-size goals or ideals and income or educational level of the household, up to certain socioeconomic levels, even when the age cohort is controlled, but these differentials are narrower than in the past (Schmidt-Sanchez, 1967). There has been a convergence toward a norm of two to four children as the ideal completed family size. Among households in the upper-income and social strata there is a tendency to put a higher valuation on children, motherhood, and the rewards of family life than there is among middle-class households. Upper-class women tend to be family-centered, to devote much time and attention to their children, and to engage to a lesser degree in labor-force activities (Scheele, 1956). At the same time, aspirations for children and for the maintenance of suitable consumption patterns can be fulfilled with less sacrifice or economic stress than that which occurs among the middle class. During the rapid economic growth which has taken place in the past two or three decades, it is the middle class which seems to have benefited most, and, at the same time, it has been subjected to the greatest strain. According to available data, the middle class has somewhat improved its relative share in the income distribution over this period. Intragenerational and intergenerational mobility has been higher than that seen among either upper- or lower-class families, which to a greater extent have remained in their respective positions. Among middle-class households there are high aspirations for children, and an extremely high valuation of education as a desirable and essential investment for the children's future, a valuation which is borne out by the strong association between education and intergenerational occupational mobility during a period in which rapid industrialization was opening up large numbers of skilled, technical white-collar jobs (Tumin and Feldman, 1961). Assessments of the number of years of education which middle-class households will provide for their children tend to be bounded by the number of years that they can afford, rather than by the number of years that the children are thought to desire or need. Among middle-class households, which have also been affected to the greatest extent by the massive out-migration to the mainland, the diffusion of North American cultural values and life-styles has been most powerful. Sociologists report a preoccupation with status and material badges of economic standing, such as housing, cars, and other durables. This group in Puerto Rico seems most closely to fit the model proposed by Leibenstein (1975), of an intense competition between numbers of children and the maintenance of status-related expenditures. Surely middle-class Puerto Rican households as a group have most harshly restricted their fertility. Presser (1973) has shown that of the three groups, the largest percentage of women of the middle class have undergone sterilization and, moreover, that they have been sterilized after the fewest years of marriage and at the lowest average parity. Underlying this phenomenon are the real socioeconomic changes which this group has undergone. The women, especially, have benefited from rising educational enrollment rates in the prewar and postwar period. They have entered the labor force in large numbers and also have switched from traditional occupations like home needlework to industrial and commercial jobs. This process has resulted in changes in family type from traditional, paternalistic, and male-dominated to a more equal partnership in which the woman has more autonomy and authority (Mintz, 1973). At the same time, the opportunity costs of the time devoted to child care by these wives have increased substantially.

Lower-class households still display the highest fertility norms, and also the greatest degree of ambivalence and inconsistency in the reporting of fertility aspirations (Hill, Stycos, and Back, 1959). The economic circumstances of many lower-income households are such as to sustain high fertility. Educational levels are relatively low, more so for women than men. Employment for women within rural areas tends to be in agriculture; and within urban areas, in domestic service and fringe service activities. Since unemployment is high, many women withdraw from the labor force. Consensual marriage is more prevalent, along with marital instability, which tends to discourage long-term planning for family welfare.

Intra- and intergenerational mobility for this class is lowest, further discouraging investment in human capital. If the research of Lewis (1966) among low-income families in San Juan can be taken as indicative of general tendencies among these groups, there is, at least from the middle-class North American perspective, a remarkable lack of parental provision for the future of children. Their concern is focused almost exclusively on providing daily food and shelter.

Traditional Puerto Rican family values remain strong for this group. Men, in particular, are concerned with the demonstration of *machismo* (virility) through sexual exploitation and the fathering of children. Equal participation of the women in important domestic decisions, including fertility decisions, is resisted, reflecting in part the fear of dependence by the male on powerful maternal figures. At the same time, the mother is idealized, and the good wife and mother is presented to women from childhood as the desirable role model. Many women escape from authoritarian parental households into early marriages or consensual unions, hoping to find some semblance of the idealized role, but, in fact, they encounter an insecure, domineering, and exploitative sexual partner. This apparently accounts for some of the ambivalence discovered by sociologists investigating attitudes toward marital roles and fertility among lower-class households.

There is little question that the efficiency of fertility regulation has been, and is, an important element in the determination of fertility in Puerto Rico. The idealization of the "good" woman as a pure being for whom discussions of sexual and contraceptive matters would be degrading has been very much a part of the cultural background in Puerto Rico. One consequence of this, reported in the research of Stycos and coauthors, has been the relatively low level of contraceptive knowledge held by most women at the time of their first marriage or sexual union (Hill, Stycos, and Back, 1959). It was found, although these data are by now somewhat dated, that a very large percentage of women knew of some contraceptive methods, but of these, the most familiar were sterilization and the condom. However, the former was inappropriate, and the latter was unacceptable to many men. Few women knew of nonpermanent methods that they themselves could control, although in the past decade knowledge of the oral contraceptive and the intrauterine device has undoubtedly modified this situation. The extreme popularity of female sterilization, a relatively drastic technique, is probably indicative of a "method problem" in Puerto Rico.

The problems of communication and the low degree of rapport between marriage partners, discovered by sociologists such as Stycos, certainly suggest difficulties in effective fertility regulation. These tend to be more severe in traditionally oriented, lower-class households, in which communication between husband and wife is more limited. Projections of their own exploitative sexual attitudes on to other men and, perhaps, feelings of guilt toward their wives lead many men to distrust the chastity and motives of their wives. This in turn makes it difficult to discuss openly the desirability of contraception, especially of female-controlled methods. Women are socialized also to feelings of shame toward their own sexual functions and organs, which further inhibits communication. Many men tend to be both proud of, and anxious about, their virility, and traditional attitudes have it that the man is the "maker" of children, while the woman is only the bearer. The man who is evidently incapable of producing children, or one who fathers only daughters, is open to ridicule. At the same time, men oftentimes view the condom with distaste as unclean and associated with recourse to prostitutes, rule out vasectomy altogether, and resist relinquishing any control over any aspect of the sexual act.

Since these patterns are prevalent among lower-class households to a greater extent, it is not surprising that they exhibit evidence of very imperfect fertility control. Women who are sterilized tend to be sterilized at older ages and at higher parities, usually after family-size norms have been exceeded. These women are likely to opt for sterilization after a history of irregular and unsuccessful experience with other methods of fertility regulation (Presser, 1973).

In summary, fertility research in Puerto Rico, buttressed by sociological and other studies, tends to suggest the applicability of a truncated form of the model outlined in chapter 2, neglecting the possibility of important supply constraints on fertility. Associated with higher levels of economic and social status are lower and more firmly held fertility goals, and changes in family behavior patterns which markedly improve the effectiveness of fertility regulation. At even higher levels of economic and social status, there is little further reduction in the unplanned fertility component, and, at the same time, there is some relaxation of the economic constraints on the demand for children and a reemergence of traditional norms favoring higher fertility. This characterization leads to expectations that the relationship between fertility and household income or economic status in Puerto Rico will be nonlinear, with the fertility response to income changes dF/dY, a rising function of household income.

THE EMPIRICAL RESULTS

As a first step in exploring this hypothesis, the sample of Puerto Rican households was divided into quartile income classes, and the relationship between fertility—measured by the number of children ever born, and household income per capita—was estimated through regression analysis across households within each total income class. The age of the mother was entered as a control, and the square of household income per capita was included in order to test for nonlinearities in the income-fertility relationship within each income class. The use of *total* household income as a stratifying variable does not bias the coefficients of household income per capita.

The use of household income per capita as the appropriate income variable rests on two considerations. Since the household is the spending unit, within which income is to a large extent pooled, household income is more appropriate than the income of the subfamily, if any, or that of the head of the household alone, as the measure of the household's current resources. Any other choice would have distorted the measure for households with several earners. Income per capita is a preferable measure, because there is a positive association of household income with household size. Single-person and small households often have low total income but relatively high incomes per capita. The use of total household income in the analysis of resource availability or income distribution would lead to serious distortion, if no correction were made for the numbers of persons sharing in that income. A further refinement would be the assignment of different weights to household members according to their ages and sexes, in order to reflect differences in consumption "requirements," but that would be beyond the scope of this research.

Table 3-5 presents the results of these preliminary regressions. Apart from the lowest-income class, neither the income nor squared income variables, which refer to total household income per capita, are significantly different from zero. In the lowest class, the positive linear and negative quadratic coefficients in income suggest a possible concave relationship over this range, as shown in figure 2-1 (page 14).

One possible objection to the use of per capita household income as the measure of resources might be that it introduces a spurious nonlinearity into the income-fertility association. With income regarded as fixed, it might be argued that there must be a high correlation between children ever born and total household size, leading to a spurious non-

Table 3-5. Income Effects on Children Ever Born by Household Income

Range of household income	Degrees of freedom	Regression coefficient			R^2
		Age	Income	Income^2	
Under $900	3934	.21 (3233)	.11 (4.4)	−0.3 (2.3)	.45
$900–$1,600	1540	.12 (838)	.138 (0.41)	−.007 (0.72)	.36
$1,700–$2,900	855	.09 (453)	.06 (0.15)	−.002 (0.32)	.35
Over $3,000	529	.06 (158)	−.01 (2.2)	.00003 (0.4)	.23

Note: Figures in parentheses are F statistics. For large sample size, the 5 percent significance level is approximately 3.9, and the 1 percent significance level is 6.4.

linear relation between children ever born and income per capita. However, the results shown in table 3-5 allay this fear, since the regression coefficients of the quadratic income terms are insignificantly different from zero, even though the range of *total* household income is restricted for each regression. As another test, a subsample was drawn of households consisting only of a husband, wife, and their own children, and the same regression was rerun, with total household income substituting for income per capita. Those results show definite nonlinearity, as can be seen in Equation 3-1:

$$CEB = -0.28 + 0.14 AGE - 0.0284 TY + 0.00006 TY^2$$
$$(.006) \qquad (.002) \qquad (.00001)$$
$$R^2 = .23 \quad (3\text{-}1)$$

The numbers in parentheses are standard errors of the coefficients. The results are consistent with the thesis of this research.

A second preliminary regression summarizes the association between cumulative fertility and household income per capita across the whole sample:

$$CEB = -1.66 + 0.16 AGE - 0.08 Y + 0.0005 Y^2 \qquad R^2 = .41$$
$$(.002) \qquad (.003) \quad (.00004) \qquad DF = 6,857$$
$$(3\text{-}2)$$

The explanatory power of Equation 3-2, and the reliability of the coefficients, are quite high. According to this preliminary estimate, the minimum of cumulative fertility occurs at an income level of about $8,000, or eight times the sample mean. Throughout, the marginal response of fertility to income changes rises with income: each $1,000 in additional income per capita is associated with an increase of 0.1 child in the response of cumulative fertility to income changes.

While this is suggestive, the estimated relationship is open to the charge of gross misspecification. To the economist, the income variable mixes wealth and price effects, fails to preserve critical distinctions among different sources of income, and omits several relevant variables correlated with income. The sociologist would concur that the income variable serves as a proxy for other aspects of socioeconomic status such as education and residential location, which are of greater relevance to demographic processes, and that the equation omits important attitudinal variables, which are not independent of household economic status.

Therefore, the rest of this chapter explores a more complete model, derived in an analogy to the stock-adjustment hypothesis discussed earlier. Since that is a theory of marital fertility, marital status must be explicitly recognized as a determinant of fertility. Then, since cumulative fertility is first analyzed, whereas the stock-adjustment theory pertains to current fertility, the duration of exposure must be considered. For women in formal marriage partnerships, the age of marriage is important; for other women, chronological age is the more appropriate measure of the duration of exposure.

In the stock-adjustment model, fertility responds to differences between desired and actual family size. Desired family size depends on two sets of variables: the determinants of preferences and norms, and the economic constraints on household choice set by wealth and opportunity costs. Norms are influenced by the community in which the household resides. Key characteristics of the community, such as its typical family size, its educational level, and its economic status, are therefore determinants of the fertility level of the individual household.

The main determinants of the price of childbearing are the opportunity costs of the mother and the average level of investment in each child, assuming that the investment per child is equal within the family. Women's opportunity costs are best measured by their educational levels and their records of labor-force participation outside the household. Investment per child is best measured by the school-enrollment rate of school-aged children within the household.

Wealth effects are captured by three income variables. For reasons already explained, the income measure relied on most heavily is the level

Table 3-6.   Variables in the Equation

Variable	B	Beta	Standard error B	F
HHYCAPSQ	0.00047	0.18653	0.00004	138.385
AGEFWM	0.15964	0.61471	0.00242	4340.627
HHYCAP	−0.08243	−0.40195	0.00326	637.617

Note: Dependent variable, CEB; Multiple R, 0.64192; R^2, 0.41206; Standard error, 2.04785; DF, 6857.

of household income per capita. To test the existence of significant non-linearities, the squared value of this measure is also related to fertility. Finally, a measure of the variability of the household's main source of income is also related to fertility. It is often hypothesized that since children provide a form of socioeconomic security, households with more secure incomes, *ceteris paribus,* would have a smaller demand for children.

In the absence of direct information on contraceptive availability, the best measure of efficiency of fertility regulation is the educational level of the wife, which has been found to be related closely to effectiveness of birth planning. Other aspects of the adjustment process, related to fecundity, are captured by the measures of chronological age. The precise definitions and identifying acronyms of all variables used in the empirical research, along with their means and standard deviations, are presented in table 3-1.

With cumulative fertility as the fertility measure, there is a problem of simultaneity involved in the interrelation of labor-force participation, educational attainment, children's enrollment rate, and fertility. In the context of life-cycle decision processes, all these, together with current marital status, are probably jointly determined. There are possible biases in the estimates of the regression coefficients due to the neglect of other simultaneous relationships between cumulative fertility and explanatory variables. However, the main purpose of this specification is to determine whether the nonlinearity in the income-fertility relationship persists when the effects of other socioeconomic variables related to fertility are taken into consideration. The general problem of simultaneity between income distribution and fertility was resolved in chapter 2, where it was found that the bias, if any, leads to underestimating the effects of income inequality on fertility.

However, there are many other interrelationships among the household characteristics included in the explanation of fertility. In particular, marital status, labor-force participation, and the school-enrollment rate of children are strongly influenced by income. Part of the influence of these variables on fertility is the indirect effect of income. On the other hand, there undoubtedly are influences on household income from women's education and labor-force participation as well. It is difficult, particularly in a life-cycle model of fertility, to specify a complete model of the relevant relationships and to find truly exogenous variables or other restrictions with which to identify the individual equations of the system.

For this reason, the two regressions discussed in this section can be regarded as bracketing equations that probably represent upper and lower bounds on the true total effect of income on fertility. The full specification implicitly assumes that the regressors are independent of one another, that there is *no* indirect effect of income on fertility working through the other household characteristics. The regression coefficients of the income variables estimated under these assumptions can probably be taken as minimal estimates of the income effects. At the other extreme, the truncated equation implicitly assumes that all the other household characteristics can be represented simply as functions of household income (that is, the underlying complete model is triangular) so that their influence can be taken entirely as an indirect effect of household income. The estimated income coefficients under this assumption are probably maximal. Consequently, although the procedures provided tests of the main hypothesis— the linearity of the income-fertility linkage—they provide only a range of plausible parameter values for that relationship.

Table 3-7 presents the results of a single-equation, ordinary least-squares regression of cumulative fertility on the full list of explanatory variables. The fit of the equation, measured by the R^2, rises to .52. The regression coefficients are all significantly different from zero at the 1 percent confidence level, and have the expected signs. The effect of marital status on fertility is naturally positive, and legal marriage results in higher fertility than does consensual marriage, other things equal. Recent labor-force participation by the woman is associated with lower fertility. The educational level of the woman is strongly associated with lower fertility. Higher levels of school enrollment for school-age children are also inversely related to fertility, reflecting the tradeoff between a large family size and an investment in the children's education. The coefficients of the neighborhood variables are interesting. They indicate that a household with given characteristics living in a high-fertility neighborhood will be likely to have distinctly higher fertility than a household with identical

Table 3-7. Regression of Children Ever Born on Full Variable List

Variable	Variables in the equation			
	B	Beta	Standard error B	F
AGEWMSQ	−0.00253	−0.59355	0.00027	90.764
AGEWM	0.27864	1.07294	0.01673	277.492
HHYCAP	−0.05720	0.27942	0.00357	256.977
HHYCSQ	0.00032	0.12841	0.00004	71.073
NEDUC	0.07953	0.08554	0.01270	39.226
NFERT	0.02951	0.14505	0.00264	125.203
LEGMAR	1.18250	0.22006	0.05850	408.572
CONMAR	0.42978	0.03328	0.11244	14.610
WRKD3Y	−0.38359	−0.06836	0.05497	48.688
EDUCWM	−0.09210	−0.15472	0.00611	226.938
ENRATE	−0.00042	−0.02716	0.00013	10.391
VARHYD	−0.00066	−0.04824	0.00012	28.158
(CONSTANT)	−3.80658			

Note: Dependent variable, CEB; Multiple R, 0.72142; R^2, 0.52045; Standard error, 1.85; DF, 6848.

characteristics living in a low-fertility neighborhood. Also, the educational level of the community seems to be positively related to the fertility of the household, with household characteristics being controlled. These results provide evidence of the force of community norms on household behavior.

Primary interest is directed to the coefficients of household income per capita and its squared value. Table 3-7 demonstrates that, although the numerical values of both coefficients are reduced by approximately 50 percent when the additional variables are introduced, both remain different from zero with an extremely high probability. The signs of the coefficients confirm the previous result that the negative impact of increased income on fertility is weakened at higher levels of income, and is transformed into a positive impact at high-income levels.

Distributional effects are clearly discernible. In figure 3-1, the estimated relationships between income and fertility under both specifications are plotted, assuming mean values of the other variables. The greater response of fertility to income changes and the greater degree of nonlinearity are apparent under the "maximum" assumption. Curves such as these could be used in combination with distributions of income to estimate the consequences of various patterns of income change. To illustrate the distributional effects more simply, maximum and minimum estimates of

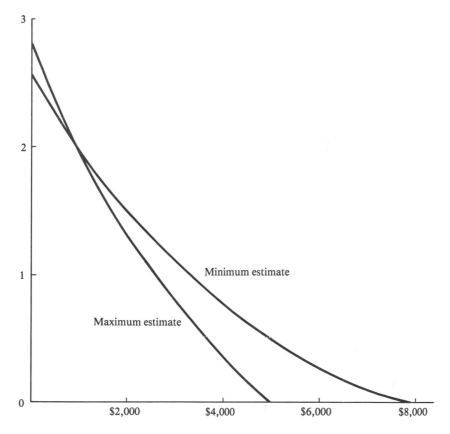

Figure 3-1. Relationship between cumulative fertility and household income per capita for mean values of other variables.

the response of cumulative fertility to an increase in household per capita income of $100 have been calculated for two household income levels: at $500 per year, which is about one-half the sample mean; and at $5,000 per year, or five times the mean. These are given below:

	Estimated $\Delta F/\Delta Y$ per year	
	At $500	At $5,000
Maximum estimate	−.075	−.033
Minimum estimate	−.037	−.017

According to both estimates, incremental income provided to low-income households would result in more than twice the fertility decline as the same increment provided to rich households, other things being equal.

Another distinct interpretation of the association between income inequality and fertility is that the degree of actual or perceived inequality in the community influences the fertility level of the individual household, apart from the household's own income. This interpretation directs attention not to the fact that the income effect on fertility is a function of income at the household level, but to the effects of inequality per se on the formation of fertility-related norms and practices. This might work through the household's aspirations for themselves and their children, for example, or through the degree to which individual households perceive and act upon social costs of rapid population growth affecting the rest of the community. One variant of this hypothesis, discussed at greater length in chapter 4, is that a high degree of socioeconomic stratification, created through inequalities in income and power, retards the diffusion of modern fertility patterns. Under this interpretation, vertical barriers to diffusion, like the horizontal barriers of ethnic, geographic, and political boundaries, perpetuate fertility differentials and retard change.

The Puerto Rican data lend themselves to an attempt to discriminate between these two hypotheses, because among the data recorded for the neighborhoods in which the household units reside is the Gini coefficient of income concentration for households of that neighborhood. This index reflects the degree of actual, and presumably perceived, inequality within what is the immediate reference group of the household. Consequently, according to this hypothesis, there should be a direct relationship between the fertility level of the individual household and the inequality index for the community, holding constant the absolute socioeconomic status of the household.

The data, however, lend absolutely no support to this interpretation. The regression coefficient of the neighborhood Gini index never reached an absolute size of even one-half its own standard error, and so never approached a level of statistical significance. The test suggests that it is evidently the extent of the household's own deprivation or economic welfare which influences its fertility, rather than perceived inequality in the society.

Other computations, not reproduced here, show the result of an attempt to discriminate among other possible sources of nonlinearity (Repetto, 1976). One possible source suggested by Willis (1973) might be an interaction between the income of the husband and the education level of the wife. As the argument runs, an educated wife is more likely to work, and so can maintain a constant opportunity cost of her time as her husband's income increases (presumably by varying her hours worked at home relative to those in the labor force), whereas the woman who is a full-time housewife must experience an increase in the opportunity cost of her time as her husband's income rises. Therefore, under this interpretation, there should be a positive interaction effect between the husband's income and the wife's education. Since educational levels of husband and wife in marital couples are positively correlated, this interaction term is also positively correlated with the square of household income. Substitution of this interaction term for the squared-income term leads to no substantial change in the statistical results. Both variables perform equally well, and so there is no opportunity to discriminate among the two hypotheses.

There is another possible source of nonlinearity, connected with the effects of the wife's education: indications from previous research suggest that the effects of the early years of a woman's education on her subsequent fertility are greater than those of the later years (Ben-Porath, 1973). Since the education of the wife is also positively correlated with household income, it is conceivable that the income-squared term might be a proxy for this variable. However, this is not the case. The coefficient of the quadratic term in the wife's education is only slightly larger than its standard error, and contributes much less to the explanation of fertility changes than does the quadratic term in income.

Yet another possible specification is that the income of the husband separately represents a wealth variable, while the income of the wife represents largely an opportunity-cost variable, while their interaction represents the same sort of process discussed by Willis (1973). While the explanatory power of this specification is also equally high, there are anomalies in the sizes and signs of the coefficients. It is fundamental to this hypothesis that the effect of husband's income on fertility, representing largely a wealth effect, should be more positive or less negative than that of the wife's income. However, the opposite is the case. Counter to the hypothesis, there does not seem to be a negative substitution effect associated with the income of the wife and a positive wealth associated with that of the husband. In summary, two of the three alternative hypotheses regarding the source of nonlinearity in the fertility equation perform *less* satisfactorily than the income distribution hypothesis, and the third— that there is an interaction effect involving husband's income and wife's education—performs equally well.

The use of children ever born in this analysis has facilitated two demonstrations: first, that the nonlinearity between income and fertility persists in a fully specified behavioral model of household fertility; and second, that this hypothesis is as consistent, or even more consistent, with the data in statistical terms than are alternative explanations of the nature of nonlinearities. There are several disadvantages to the measure of cumulative fertility in this context, however. There are important simultaneous interactions between lifetime fertility and other decision variables, and this leads to problems of estimation and model specification. Also, it is reflective of past behavior, while the explanatory variables include indicators of current household and community characteristics. Consequently, in situations of rapid socioeconomic change, these may be only weakly reflective of the value of those variables at the time when the fertility decisions were made. Also, from the perspective of the present research, the underlying model of fertility as a stock-adjustment process clearly calls for the use of current fertility as the dependent variable. Use of current fertility also reduces simultaneity problems, because more of the women's characteristics, like educational attainment, past labor-force participation, and marital status become predetermined in this context.

Unfortunately, while the Puerto Rican census contains direct information for each respondent woman on the number of children ever born, it does not contain direct information on recent fertility events. As a result, it was necessary to construct the best possible measure of current fertility for each woman in the sample. This measure is the number of her own children in the household who are two years old or younger. It was advisable to examine births within the past two years rather than within one year in order to reduce distortions resulting from age misreporting. The main difficulty with this fertility measure, of course, is that it confounds fertility with infant mortality. Children are not counted who were born but died within the two years prior to the census. Although infant mortality is not high in Puerto Rico, it is differentially distributed, so that some errors are involved in the use of this measure. It should be kept in mind that the measure probably understates, in relative terms, the fertility of lower-income households.

Investigation of current fertility calls for a change in the basic model. Because of the pronounced nonlinearity of age-specific rates, which mark the bunching in time of marriage, family formation, and the loss of fecundity, a quadratic term in the age of the woman had to be inserted into the model. A negative sign is expected for the coefficient of this variable. Furthermore, the underlying stock-adjustment model calls for the inclusion of the existing stock of children as a determinant of current

Table 3-8. Regression of Current Fertility on Full Variable List

	Variables in the equation			
Variable	B	Beta	Standard error B	F
CEB2PLUS	−0.01372	−0.08518	0.00257	28.409
AGEWMSQ	−0.00061	−0.90073	0.00006	116.548
AGEWM	0.03062	0.74524	0.00359	72.797
HHYCAP	−0.00550	0.16983	0.00077	51.698
HHYCSQ	0.00003	0.07673	0.00001	14.136
NEDUC	0.00904	0.06146	0.00269	11.328
NFERT	0.00277	0.08600	0.00056	24.355
LEGMAR	0.28904	0.33994	0.01257	529.150
CONMAR	0.03627	0.01775	0.02375	2.331
WRKD3Y	0.02327	0.02620	0.01165	3.987
EDUCWM	−0.00298	−0.03164	0.00131	5.165
ENRATE	−0.00010	−0.04057	0.00003	13.019
VARHYD	−0.00001	−0.00427	0.00003	0.123
(CONSTANT)	−0.31629			

Note: Dependent variable, CLT2; Multiple R, 0.38329; R^2, 0.14691; Standard error, 0.39060; DF, 6847.

fertility rates. This stock was directly measured as the number of children older than two years who were alive in the family, thus avoiding the biases associated with the usual substitution of a lagged value of the dependent variable into the regression equation. Other things being equal, including the demand for children and the effectiveness of fertility regulation, an inverse relationship would be expected between current fertility and the stock of children already alive. An alternative hypothesis—that fertility differentials among women are attributable to persistent differences in fecundity or contraceptive efficiency—would lead to the expectation that the association would be positive.

Table 3-8 presents the basic empirical test of this model on the entire sample of almost 7,000 women. Since there is an econometric problem of heteroskedasticity in the error terms, introduced by the use of a virtually binary dependent variable, supplementary regression analysis was carried out, involving the use of weights derived from the predicted fertility values of the equation (see table 3-8). The results, not reported here, are the same in all main conclusions as the ordinary least-squares regressions.

In these regressions, the hypothesis of a linear relationship between income and fertility is decisively rejected, in favor of a U-shaped curve, as before. The results also give support to the stock-adjustment hypothesis: the number of children alive in the household is linked to lower current fertility, other things being equal. In addition, the effects of age and marital status on fertility are strong: fertility is much higher in legal than in consensual unions. Among the price variables, the negative association between school-enrollment rates and fertility is prominent, while the negative effect of women's educational attainment is barely different from zero; and the labor-force participation variable is of the wrong sign, but not significantly different from zero. The influence of community characteristics on individual household behavior remains evident: households residing in communities with higher fertility tend to have higher current fertility than similar households in low-fertility neighborhoods. Viewing the results in an overall perspective, they seem to lend strong support to both the stock-adjustment model and to the importance of distributional influences on fertility, and at the same time, they seem to be consistent with other known relationships between socioeconomic variables and current fertility.

It has been suggested that effective control over fertility does not require that the couple control each and every birth, but only that the couple make decisions at the margin; for example, whether to have a third or fourth child, if these represent the marginal children for them. Consequently, it was thought desirable to investigate separately the fertility behavior of low-parity, medium-parity, and high-parity women. In order to do this, the sample of legally married women was split into those with zero to three children ever born, four to seven children ever born, and eight children or more. Since the stratifying variable, parity, is not the same as the measure of current fertility, this can be done without bias. The results of the basic regressions, run separately on each of these subsamples, are reported in tables 3-9, 3-10, and 3-11.

The results are interesting. As hypothesized, the systematic component of the fertility of medium-parity women, as measured by the R^2 of the explanatory equation, is substantially greater than that of either high- or low-parity women. Within each parity group, the income distribution effect on fertility is statistically significant, and in the same direction as before. Also, within each subsample, strong support is registered for the stock-adjustment hypothesis. The sign of the coefficient of the stock of children already alive is in each regression negative and significant. Among medium-parity women, the negative impact of children's school-enrollment rates is quite strong. There is also a discernible positive impact

Table 3-9. Regression of Current Fertility: Low-Parity Women

Variable	Variables in the equation			
	B	Beta	Standard error B	F
CEB2PLUS	−0.14709	−0.32169	0.00988	221.638
AGEWM	0.01765	0.30188	0.00847	4.344
AGEWMSQ	−0.00042	−0.46254	0.00013	10.662
HHYCAP	−0.00910	−0.28285	0.00127	51.547
HHYCSQ	0.00004	0.12124	0.00001	12.923
NEDUC	0.01766	0.10123	0.00517	11.680
NFERT	0.00273	0.06558	0.00115	5.676
WRKD3Y	−0.01401	−0.01375	0.02046	0.469
EDUCWM	0.00102	0.00865	0.00258	0.156
ENRATE	0.00001	0.00203	0.00005	0.013
VARYHD	−0.00027	−0.7796	0.00007	17.330
(CONSTANT)	0.29601			

Note: Dependent variable, CLT2; Sample, legally married women with CEB 0–3; Multiple R, 0.43875; R^2, 0.19250; Standard error, 0.45580; DF, 2533.

Table 3-10. Regression of Current Fertility: Medium-Parity Women

Variable	Variables in the equation			
	B	Beta	Standard error B	F
CEB2PLUS	−0.16411	−0.38421	0.01261	169.383
AGEWM	−0.05628	−0.81252	0.01865	9.106
AGEWMSQ	0.00057	0.58775	0.000026	4.806
HHYCAP	−0.01302	−0.19476	0.00477	7.453
HHYCSQ	0.00023	0.12346	0.00012	3.584
NEDUC	−0.00421	−0.02343	0.00784	0.289
NFERT	0.00365	0.09475	0.00158	5.346
WRKD3Y	−0.01599	−0.01397	0.03311	0.233
EDUCWM	0.00710	0.062661	0.00374	3.596
ENRATE	−0.00025	−0.11874	0.00006	18.449
VARHYD	−0.00005	−0.01658	0.00009	9.353
(CONSTANT)	2.40476			

Note: Dependent variable, CLT2; Sample, legally married women with CEB 4–7; Multiple R, 0.57831; R^2, 0.33444; Standard error, 0.41497; DF, 916.

of the community's educational standards and fertility norms. Work experience and the woman's own educational background are generally insignificantly related to current fertility, when other variables are controlled.

Among low- and high-parity women there is a significant negative association between current fertility and a variable which serves as an

Table 3-11. Regression of Current Fertility: High-Parity Women

Variable	Variables in the equation			
	B	Beta	Standard error B	F
CEB2PLUS	−0.08854	−0.25588	0.01826	23.504
AGEWM	−0.04083	−0.45369	0.04885	0.698
AGEWMSQ	0.00023	0.19915	0.00063	0.135
HHYCAP	−0.03171	−0.36478	0.01002	10.008
HHYCSQ	0.00030	0.29594	0.00011	7.020
NEDUC	0.02252	0.08744	0.01737	1.682
NFERT	0.00657	0.15384	0.00285	5.336
WRKD3Y	0.14889	0.08815	0.08478	3.084
EDUCWM	0.00868	0.05634	0.00793	1.200
ENRATE	−0.00008	−0.03529	0.00010	0.524
VARYHD	−0.00055	−0.17232	0.00016	11.817
(CONSTANT)	2.21977			

Note: Dependent variable, CLT2; Sample, legally married women with CEB 8+; Multiple R, 0.48949; R^2, 0.23960; Standard error, 0.49274; DF, 329.

estimate of the *variability* of the husband's income. In the cross-sectional census sample of households, there is no direct information, naturally, on the variability of the individual worker's income over time. Therefore, an indirect estimate was constructed by measuring the sample variance, across all workers in the sample, of the income of men in the same job. The job was defined in terms of three categories—industry, occupation, and class of worker. As a simple approximating assumption, it was estimated that the variance of income from any man's job was the *sum* of three components: the variance in income of all workers in the same sector; the variance of all workers in the same occupation; and the variance in income of all workers in the same employment class. Thus, the estimated variance of a self-employed insurance salesman's income would be the sum of the variances of incomes in the financial sector, of incomes of salesmen and those in related occupations, and of self-employed workers. This estimating procedure involves heroic assumptions regarding the absence of covariance among incomes in these categories. However, it is possibly a useful procedure for the construction of an ordinal index of income variance among different workers. Since real interest attaches only to the sign of the association between income variance and fertility, an adequate ordinal ranking of income variability might be sufficient.

The predicted association was positive, since children, particularly sons, are widely supposed to be regarded by parents as assets, and a form of intrafamily insurance against social or economic disaster and a source of assistance in the older years. Surprisingly, the association proved to be consistently negative, and significantly different from zero in most regression equations. Higher-income variability tends in Puerto Rico to be associated with lower fertility, other things being equal. Those men who work in jobs with uncertain income prospects tend to have wives with lower current and lifetime fertility, other things (including current income) being held constant.

This finding concludes the examination of Puerto Rican census data. The data consistently support the hypothesis that a more equal income distribution would be associated with lower overall fertility. The statistical results consistently support the predictions of the model.

REFERENCES

Ben-Porath, Yoram. 1973. "Fertility in Israel: Point and Counterpoint," *Journal of Political Economy* vol. 81, no. 2, pt. 2 (suppl., March/April) pp. 202–233.

Davis, Kingsley. 1973. "Foreword," in Harriet Presser, *Sterilization and Fertility Decline in Puerto Rico,* Population Monograph Series, no. 13 (Berkeley, University of California).

Hill, Reuben, J. Mayone Stycos, and Kurt W. Back. 1959. *The Family and Population Control* (Chapel Hill, N.C., University of North Carolina Press).

Ingram, John C. 1962. *Regional Payments Mechanisms: The Case of Puerto Rico* (Chapel Hill, N.C., University of North Carolina Press).

Joseph, Scott. 1967. "Sources of Social Change in Community, Family, and Fertility in a Puerto Rican Town," *American Journal of Sociology* vol. 72, no. 5 (March) pp. 520–530.

Leibenstein, Harvey. 1975. "The Economic Theory of Fertility Decline," *Quarterly Journal of Economics* vol. 89, no. 1 (February) pp. 1–31.

Lewis, Gordon K. 1963. *Puerto Rico: Freedom and Power in the Caribbean* (New York, Monthly Review Press).

Lewis, Oscar. 1966. *La Vida: A Puerto Rican Family in the Culture of Poverty* (New York, Random House).

Mintz, Sydney. 1973. "An Essay in the Definition of National Culture," in F. Cordasco and E. Buccione, eds., *The Puerto Rican Experience* (Totowa, N.J., Rowman and Littlefield).

Presser, Harriet. 1973. *Sterilization and Fertility Decline in Puerto Rico,* Population Monograph Series, No. 13 (Berkeley, University of California).

Repetto, Robert. 1976. "Inequality and the Birth Rate in Puerto Rico: Evidence From Household Census Data," Research paper no. 14 (June) (Cambridge, Mass., Center for Population Studies, Harvard University).

Reynolds, Lloyd G., and Peter Gregory. 1965. *Wages, Productivity, and Industrialization in Puerto Rico* (New Haven, Conn., Yale University Press).

Sandis, Eva. 1970. "Characteristics of Puerto Rican Migrants to, and from, the United States," *International Migration Review* vol. 4, no. 2, pp. 22–39.

Scheele, Raymond. 1956. "The Prominent Families of Puerto Rico," in Julian Steward, ed., *The People of Puerto Rico* (Urbana, University of Illinois Press).

Schmidt-Sanchez, Carlos. 1967. "Changing Patterns of Population Fertility in Puerto Rico" (Ph.D. dissertation, University of Illinois, Urbana).

Stycos, J. Mayone. 1955. *Family and Fertility in Puerto Rico* (New York, Columbia University Press).

Tumin, Melvin, and Arnold Feldman. 1961. *Social Class and Social Change in Puerto Rico* (Princeton, N.J., Princeton University Press).

Vazquez, Jose. 1968. "Fertility Decline in Puerto Rico: Extent and Causes," *Demography* vol. 5, no. 2, pp. 855–865.

Weisskopf, Richard. 1970. "Income Distribution and Economic Growth in Puerto Rico, Argentina, and Mexico" (New Haven, Conn., Yale University, Economic Growth Center) Mimeo.

Willis, Robert. 1973. "A New Approach to the Economic Theory of Fertility Behavior," *Journal of Political Economy* vol. 81, no. 2, pt. 2 (suppl., March/April) pp. 514–564.

4 ⌐⌐ KOREA AS A CASE STUDY: AN HISTORICAL APPROACH

INTRODUCTION AND SUMMARY

The experience of the Republic of Korea in the postwar period provides a valuable case study of the influence of widely shared and rapid economic development on fertility. Within the span of a decade, from about 1944 to 1954, Korea suffered a series of shattering events. It emerged as a society in which economic as well as social distinctions had been leveled to an extent which probably surpassed that in any non-Communist country. In fact, the distribution of income at the end of this period is one of the most equal in any nation for which measures are available. Moreover, the pattern of Korean growth in the postwar period, based on intensive use of human resources with widespread access to education, has preserved a great deal of that equality.

This high degree of equality was achieved not through a particularly strong commitment to popular welfare, but through the disruption and devastation of war; through a land reform which was legislated in an atmosphere of fear of Communist intervention and carried through mostly by private land sales or by the U.S. military government; and through an education reform which was also initiated by the U.S. military government. Since 1953 there has been no significant redistribution.

Korea provides a distinctive model among less-developed countries which have undergone a substantial fertility decline. Economic policy has emphasized very rapid growth that relies heavily on imported capital and technology, the relative neglect (until recently) of agriculture in favor of nontraditional manufacturing industries producing goods for export, and a minimum of welfare programs of any kind. Economic equality has been preserved mainly by the growth of labor demand, which has expanded employment opportunities and raised real wages. Moreover, the political orientation of the Korean government cannot be said to foster decentralization or popular participation.

Still, the fertility decline in Korea between 1960 and 1974 has been one of the fastest recorded in any nation in history. This suggests that what may be essential is improvement in the living standards and opportunities of the poor majority, and the absence of wide socioeconomic disparities, rather than a particular political orientation of the government.

The reason that the fertility decline in Korea was so fast is because it was so pervasive. Birth rates started to decline at about the same time in all regions, classes, and categories of households. Within six years from the onset of the transition, fertility differentials between groups had begun to narrow, and within a decade there was substantial convergence. Shifts in the female population—from rural to urban, uneducated to educated, or economically inactive to employed—were important but by no means the predominant influences on fertility. Among the uneducated, the rural, and those within the traditional sector, birth rates also fell. Such broad participation in demographic change is characteristic of societies without marked cultural and socioeconomic differentiation.

Equally broad were the mechanisms of fertility decline. The spread of contraception was only one means of fertility control, and, in the first five years, a relatively unimportant one. Recourse to abortion and delayed marriage were more significant. It is impossible to disentangle the effects of marriage at an older age, the increasing incidence of abortion, and a more widespread use of contraceptives obtained from private sources and from the national family-planning program, because the impact of all of these are mutually interdependent. The evidence implies that all were important. Even in rural areas the decline cannot be attributed mainly to the success of the government's family-planning program.

Econometric analysis of recent Korean fertility leads to similar conclusions. The relation of household fertility to these socioeconomic conditions—taking into account indirect influences which operate through marriage patterns, desired family size, attitudes and aspirations toward children, and contraceptive practice—are such that greater equality in the distribution of income and broader participation in the development process are conducive to lower fertility.

THE PATTERN OF ECONOMIC DEVELOPMENT

The disappearance of the Japanese colonial administrators and businessmen in 1944, and the discrediting of many of the Korean colonial elite as collaborators, removed the top layer of Korean society. The land reform destroyed the economic and social base of the *yangban*, the traditional elite, while creating a rural pattern of equal small owner-operators. The return of millions of Koreans from abroad and from North Korea created an urbanized and socially undifferentiated society. The uprooting of nearly a quarter of the Korean population during the civil war destroyed what was left of the traditional family and village organization, and put a premium on individual advancement and the nuclear household. The economic disruption of the period put households under extreme economic hardship, broke up families, and delayed marriages. The exposure of the population to Western ideas, a westernized military, and the U.S. military government created a new ideology of equal opportunity. The rapid introduction of universal primary education opened the path to socioeconomic advancement which had previously been limited to an elite.

Culturally homogeneous to start with, postwar Korea emerged as an extremely open and egalitarian society. The description written by Douglas (1962), an astute observer of the period, cannot be bettered:

Korea today comes close to having no class structure at all. . . . Fifty years ago Korea did have a simple class structure, featuring nobles and peasants. The position of the nobility was based on land ownership, government jobs, or both. The peasants did the work. Since then the trials of Korea have hopelessly jumbled the picture. The Japanese rule destroyed the position of some nobles, enhanced that of others, created some workers and middle-class families, but. did not build a modern class structure. The American military occupation and the post-war land reform changed the situation even more, depriving most of the noble class of the land on which its economic power was based. Then came the influx of millions of refugees from the North, where some had been rich, some poor, and some in-between. They had varying degrees of success in re-establishing themselves, and their success did not necessarily correspond to their former social position. Then came the Korean War, which again moved masses of people back and forth, and capriciously made some men millionaires and destroyed the entire economic holding or even the lives of others. By the end of the War any clear class pattern had been destroyed.

The degree and sources of economic equality can be specified in more detail. Table 4-1 shows a number of estimates of the distribution of

Table 4-1. Estimates of Income Distribution for the Republic of Korea

| | Reference year | | | | | | | | |
| | 1966 | 1966 | 1968 | 1969 | 1970 | 1970 | 1970 | 1971 | 1971 |
Spending unit	Per household	Per household	Per household	Per household	Per individual	Per household	Per household	Per household	Per household
Percentage of population					**Percentage of Income**				
0–10	3.9	2.3	3.6	3.4	2.4	3.1	2.5	2.9	4.2
10–20	5.5	4.2	5.0	5.0	3.7	4.0	4.0	4.3	5.7
20–30	6.4	5.4	6.0	6.0	4.6	4.8	5.0	5.2	6.5
30–40	7.4	6.5	6.8	7.0	5.5	5.8	6.0	6.3	7.3
40–50	8.4	7.8	7.9	8.1	6.7	7.0	7.0	7.3	8.2
50–60	9.4	9.2	9.0	9.2	8.1	8.2	8.4	8.5	9.1
60–70	10.8	10.9	10.3	10.6	9.7	10.0	9.9	10.0	10.2
70–80	12.4	13.1	12.2	12.5	12.2	12.5	12.0	12.1	11.6
80–90	14.8	16.3	15.0	15.2	16.1	16.5	15.6	15.3	13.9
90–100	21.0	24.3	24.2	23.0	31.0	28.0	29.6	28.1	23.3
95–100	12.1	14.1	14.8	13.7	20.1	17.1	19.4	19.4	14.8
Note: Statistics of interest:									
Gini coefficient	.2650	.3416	.3045	.2982	.4065	.3719	.3836	.3601	.2718
Kuznets index	.2000	.2589	.2295	.2242	.3095	.2874	.2884	.2705	.2011
E-entropy	.1111	.1801	.1492	.1404	.2576	.2139	.2339	.2079	.1259
Mean income	N.A.	N.A.	255,240	295,800	N.A.	N.A.	N.A.	448,000	400,000
GNP per capita in won	35,480	35,480	51,715	65,740	79,935	79,935	79,935	96,190	96,190

Source: Shail Jain, *Size Distribution of Income: A Compilation of Data* (Washington, D.C., World Bank, 1975) p. 65.

Table 4-2.   Percentage Distribution of Cultivated Area in Korea, by Size of Farm

Farm size (in ha)	1945	1955	1960	1965	1970	1973
Under 0.3		5.8	5.3	3.8	3.4	3.4
0.3–0.5	10.4	12.2	11.4	8.6	7.3	8.0
0.5–1.0		29.2	27.9	26.7	27.8	26.9
1.0–2.0	Not more than 40.0	35.9	37.0	40.5	40.6	41.4
2.0–3.0	Not more than 40.0	15.9	17.3	15.3	13.6	13.3
Over 3.0	More than 26.4	1.0	1.2	5.1	7.3	7.0

Source: Republic of Korea, Ministry of Agriculture, *Yearbook of Agriculture and Forestry Statistics* (Seoul, 1968, pp. 46–47; and 1974, pp. 28–29); and Ki Hyuk Pak and others, *A Study of Land Tenure System in Korea* (Seoul, Korea Land Economics Research System, 1966) p. 92. The break point in the 1945 figures is 5 chongbo (1 chongbo = 0.992 ha) rather than 3, so the actual 1–3 ha figure would be lower than that shown in table 4-2 while the over 3 ha percentage would be larger.

incomes among households in Korea for the 1960s and 1970s. While each one is questionable, the general pattern is consistent. By these estimates, which refer to a period at least a decade after the close of the period of disruption and leveling, Korea was still one of the most egalitarian economies in the world. The distribution of income and ownership shortly after the end of the Korean War must have been more equal still.

The reasons for this exceptional degree of equality are not hard to find. Most of them stem from the equal distribution of earning assets. In the rural sector, the main factor was the thorough land reform which took place. That this program was successful in terms of its objectives of limiting farm size and transferring ownership to the cultivator is unquestionable. The fraction of farm household heads who were tenants, which had grown to 56 percent in 1938, fell to 5 percent after the reform (Ban and coauthors, 1979), and the fraction who were full owners rose from 19 percent in 1938 to 72 percent after the reform. About 40 percent of farm households were raised from the status of landless tenants to owners, and another 20 percent or so had their own holdings augmented by the conversion of tenancies (M. G. Lee, 1976). The distribution of agricultural holdings also became much more equal, as table 4-2 shows.

The redistribution of farm income implied by these changes was substantial (Cho, 1964). Rents, about one-quarter of farm income, were redistributed from the landlord class (about 4 percent of the farm population) to the bottom 80 percent of farmers who previously had been tenants or part-tenants. The equality that was introduced in the agrarian

Table 4-3.   The Educational Status of the Korean Male
Population, 1955

Educational status	No.	Percentage of total	Percentage of those not in school
Total male population	10,967	100.0	
Attending school	2,354	.21	—
Primary school	1,898	.17	(.22)
Middle school	553	.05	(.06)
High school	178	.02	(.02)
University	106	.01	(.01)
Not in school	8,613	.89	(100.0)

Source: Republic of Korea, Economic Planning Board, *Korea
Statistical Yearbook* (Seoul, 1962) pp. 22–23.

structure has persisted. Holdings in excess of 3 ha had grown only to 7 percent of the cultivated area by 1973, and the large bulk of farmland is in
small holdings of 0.5 to 2 ha. The rural economy of Korea is one of substantially equal peasant farmers.

In the urban economy, perhaps the main instrument of equalization
was the destruction of war. During and after World War II, the industrial
plant created by the Japanese deteriorated badly. These losses, however,
were dwarfed by the destruction wrought by the Korean War. In addition to wartime casualties, estimated at more than 1.5 million persons,
property damage has been estimated as equal to 30 and 40 percent of
the total capital stock (Brown, 1973, page 35). Also, hyperinflation
destroyed the value of financial assets. Prices rose by 350 percent in 1946,
550 percent in 1951, and 115 percent in 1952 (Cole and Lyman, 1971,
page 25). This rapid and unanticipated devaluation of financial assets
further reduced concentration of wealth, since the distribution of financial assets in the population was quite unequal. Most of the forced savings
from inflation were expended in government operations, mainly military.

The other major element in the creation of such a high degree of
equality in the Korean economy in 1955 was the very equal distribution
of human capital. Formal education is one element. As table 4-3 shows,
less than 10 percent of the out-of-school male population had gone beyond primary school. This represents a very equal distribution of a very
limited educational stock at that time. Furthermore, the fact that such a
large fraction of the working population were recent migrants and refugees, and so much of the economic activity had been started afresh after
the conflict, implies that the working population were equally placed with

regard to on-the-job skills, entrenched position, and other nonformal aspects of occupational advantage. The urban influx between 1945–55, which raised the percentage of the population living in cities from 14 percent to 24 percent, consisted largely of people with limited skills and capital who had to start from scratch.

Despite the absence of fully satisfactory data on which to base a conclusion, the consensus of opinion is that the process of economic growth in Korea during the years of rapid expansion, 1963–75, preserved much of the initial equality in the distribution of economic welfare. The various estimates of income distribution, shown in table 4-1, are consistent with this. It was not through any particular welfare orientation in government policies that this was achieved. Indeed, economic policy was dedicated to rapid growth using external resources, market processes, and a minimum of welfare measures. The key element in preserving equality was the rapid growth of labor demand, which drew potential workers (especially women) into the labor force, reduced unemployment and underemployment, pulled workers out of the low-productivity agricultural sector, and led to substantial increases in real wages during the second half of the period.

In addition, it appears that the distribution of earnings among workers in the urban sector has become, if anything, less concentrated. Earnings differentials between skilled and unskilled occupations have narrowed (IBRD, 1976), and the income and consumption levels of wage earners have increased relative to those of salary earners (Abraham, 1976). These changes are attributable in part to the rapid growth and diffusion of education in the labor force.

In the rural sector, reasonably complete data, summarized in table 4-4, indicate an equal and unchanging distribution of income. The share of the lowest 40 percent of farm households in total farm income has gone from 20 percent in 1963 to 19 percent in 1974. The fact that this relatively high share of income goes to the lower strata does not even fully reflect the actual degree of equality, since farm households on larger holdings tend to have more members.

During the 1960s, the disparity between rural and urban incomes widened, which implies greater concentration overall. The widening gap stemmed from the faster growth of output and productivity in the urban sector, and adverse movements in the terms of trade against agriculture. Since 1969, because of government price policies for major crops, there has been a substantial improvement in the farmer's terms of trade, equivalent approximately to a 10 percent increment to farm income annually

Table 4-4.   Distribution of Farm Household Income in Korea,
for Selected Years

Percentage distribution	1963	1967	1970	1974
Top 10	31	24	—	25
Top 20	44	40	39	41
Next 40	36	40	40	40
Next 30	17	17	18	16
Bottom 10	3	3.5	3	3

Source: Sung Hwan Ban, Pal Yong Moon, Dwight H. Perkins,
Vincent Brandt, Albert Keitel, and John Sloboda, *Studies in the
Modernization of the Republic of Korea, 1945–1975: Rural Develop-
ment*, Harvard East Asian Monograph no. 89 (Cambridge, Mass.,
Council on East Asian Studies, Harvard University, 1979).

since 1970 (Ban and coauthors, 1979). This has led to a reversal and
narrowing of the rural-urban gap.

This sketch of Korean development depicts a process of very rapid
growth and change, which has preserved an unusually egalitarian social
and economic structure. It is noteworthy that the initial equalization came
about through wartime destruction of assets and a postwar land reform
which was strongly stimulated by outside forces. The postwar experience
has been characterized neither by a strong government commitment to
the welfare of the poor majority nor by a high degree of popular participation in political life. In intention and effect, economic policy has been
dedicated to rapid growth in the nontraditional sector, relying heavily
on external capital and technology. Despite this, the rapid growth of labor
demand, combined with equal initial distribution of, and access to formal
education, has kept large disparities from emerging. Moreover, from the
standpoint of this study, it is important to note that demographic factors
other than migration have been relatively insignificant in creating or
preserving the egalitarian structure. Any causal relationship clearly runs
from the socioeconomic structure to fertility change, not the reverse. The
following sections will explore the consequences of this development pattern on the evolution of fertility.

THE PATTERN OF FERTILITY DECLINE

Fertility Trends and Patterns of Change.   From 1960 to 1974, the
crude birth rate in Korea fell from 41 to 24, a decline of 41 percent. This

Table 4-5. Countries in Which Fertility Has Declined Appreciably for Selected Years

Country	Crude birth rates				Percentage changes	
	1960	1965	1970	1974	1965–74	1960–74
Africa						
Egypt	43.6	42.1	39.4	34.8	17.3	20.1
Mauritius	40.0	35.9	28.7	25.1	30.1	37.2
Tunisia	46.6	44.7	41.4	36.0	19.4	22.8
Latin America						
Barbados	30.70	26.8	22.8	20.8	22.5	32.2
Chile	36.6	32.8	28.9	23.2	29.3	36.5
Colombia	45.3	44.2	42.1	33.0	24.4	27.2
Costa Rica	46.6	41.1	35.4	28.0	31.8	39.9
Cuba	32.4	33.1	30.2	25.3	23.5	22.0
Dominican Republic	48.5	47.2	46.4	37.5	20.6	22.7
El Salvador	48.4	46.1	43.2	40.3	12.6	16.7
Jamaica	39.4	38.5	35.3	30.6	20.5	22.3
Mexico	45.2	43.7	42.4	40.0	8.5	11.4
Panama	41.2	39.8	37.3	31.0	22.1	24.8
Trinidad and Tobago	37.7	32.5	26.6	24.0	26.2	36.2
Venezuela	45.4	42.1	37.8	36.0	14.5	20.8
Asia and the Pacific						
China	30.8	34.0	27.4	26.0	23.5	15.6
Fiji	42.0	35.7	28.5	28.0	21.6	34.1
Hong Kong	34.7	28.3	21.4	18.3	35.4	47.2
India	44.0	42.6	40.6	36.0	15.5	18.2
Indonesia	46.9	45.9	43.9	40.0	12.8	14.7
Korea	40.6	35.1	30.1	24.0	31.6	40.8
Malaysia	45.0	42.2	33.9	31.4	25.6	30.2
Philippines	44.5	44.2	44.0	37.5	15.2	15.8
Singapore	37.8	29.4	23.0	17.6	40.2	53.4
Sri Lanka	35.6	33.1	30.0	27.2	17.8	23.7
Taiwan	39.4	33.0	26.8	23.0	30.4	41.6
Thailand	46.1	44.3	43.6	34.0	23.0	26.2
Turkey	42.8	40.6	39.7	34.0	16.2	20.7
Vietnam	41.5	41.5	41.4	32.0	22.9	22.9

Source: Parker Mauldin and Bernard Berelson, "Cross-Cultural Review of the Effectiveness of Family Planning Programs" (Liege, Belgium, International Union for the Scientific Study of Population, 1976).

is one of the fastest declines ever recorded (Mauldin and Berelson, 1976). Table 4-5 compares the Korean experience with that of other less-developed countries which recorded substantial declines over this period. Aside from Hong Kong and Singapore, the greatest reductions were in Taiwan and Korea, at virtually the same rate. These countries, which have recently begun the fertility transition, have undergone more rapid rates of change than did developed countries in which fertility is now already low. The "new demographic transition" is proceeding at a faster rate than the earlier one (Kirk, 1971). So, Korea's rate of decline is not only one of the fastest among developing countries, it is one of the fastest in all history.

A part of this exceptional performance can be explained in terms of the peculiar historic circumstances of the period. In 1960 the postwar baby boom was just coming to an end. The fertility descent in 1960 began from an unusually high level, caused by the "bunching" of childbirths at the end of the 1950s to couples whose family formation had been delayed or interrupted by the war. A study of cohort fertility shows that the cohorts of women aged nineteen to twenty-eight in 1950 display atypical bimodal patterns of age-specific fertility, with the major peak fertility rates being attained relatively late, when the women were in their early thirties (Nam-Il Kim 1977). The lifetime fertility of these cohorts, however, did not differ greatly from those of cohorts just preceding or following. Because of this disturbance in the timing of births, changes in period fertility rates over the decade 1960–70 decline about 25 percent, while cohort rates fall by 15 percent to 20 percent. Table 4-6 shows the decline in period rates during the postwar years.

A decomposition analysis, summarized in table 4-7, indicates the main features of the decline: the predominant influence of rising age at marriage and abortion in the period until 1966, and the growing significance of contraception within marriage thereafter. Changing age-sex composition has contributed little to the change in the crude birth rate in Korea as a whole, but the selectivity of urban migration has contributed substantially to the narrowing of urban-rural birth rates.

Also evident in the pattern of fertility change is the narrowing of fertility differentials by socioeconomic status and residence after 1966. Since that date, there has been rapid convergence of fertility, due largely to the diffusion of contraceptive practice to formerly high-fertility populations and to the narrowing of differentials in age at marriage.

The narrowing of these differentials is important. Most theories of fertility emphasize compositional changes in the population: from rural to urban, or farm to nonfarm; from uneducated to more educated; from extended to nuclear households, and so on. However, recent reevaluations of the demographic transition in Europe have demonstrated that these structural shifts have only been responsible for part of the decline. The rest was due to fertility reductions within high-fertility subgroups, that is, among rural women, uneducated women, and women not in the

Table 4-6. Age-Specific Fertility Rates (ASFR) and Age-Specific
Marital Fertility Rates (ASMFR), in Korea, 1955–75
(per thousand)

	1955–60	1960–65	1965–70	1970–75
ASFR				
15–19	38	20	12	10
20–24	308	255	180	146
25–29	335	351	309	301
30–34	270	277	223	220
35–39	194	189	134	88
40–44	96	92	59	19
45–49	18	17	10	7
ASMFR				
15–19	357	356	350	387
20–24	440	443	394	431
25–29	367	383	346	342
30–34	298	295	237	231
35–39	221	212	148	96
40–44	117	111	71	22
45–49	24	22	13	9

Source: Tai Hwan Kwon, "The Historical Background to
Korea's Demographic Transition," in Robert Repetto, Kwon
Tai Hwan, Kim Song Ung, Peter Donaldson, and Kim Dae
Young, *Economic Development, Population Policy, and the
Demographic Transition in the Republic of Korea* (Cambridge,
Mass., Harvard Institute of International Development, 1978).

labor force. The onset of the transition was generally later for these high-fertility subgroups, though, and the pace of fertility decline was slower. As a result, fertility differentials opened up, widened, and persisted for a long time. In some European countries—Germany, for example—differentials widened for fifty years and persisted for a century (Knodel, 1974).

It is clear that the overall pace of fertility change depends not only on the extent of compositional shifts in the percentage of the population in various fertility-related subgroups, but also on the extent of fertility decline *within* each of these subgroups. In the older European demographic transition, there is some evidence that socioeconomic fertility differentials converged earlier in those regions—like Scandinavia—in which the social structure was more integrated, and class barriers less rigid (Bendix and Lipset, 1966).

This hypothesis seems to illuminate the Korean experience. What is remarkable about Korea's fertility decline is its pervasiveness. In other

Table 4-7. Components of Changes of Crude Birth Rates and Total Fertility Rates in Korea

	Crude birth rate (%)				Total fertility rate (%)			
	1955–60	1960–65	1965–70	1970–75	1955–60	1960–65	1965–70	1970–75
Total actual change	2.6	−19.2	−16.9	−10.5	5.6	−16.8	−17.6	−13.4
Changes								
Due to age-specific fertility rate	4.2	−17.1	−16.6	−12.0	5.6	−16.8	−17.6	−13.4
Due to age-specific marital fertility rate	9.2	−9.8	−10.8	−8.9	9.5	−10.5	−14.1	−9.9
Contraceptives	—	−1.5	−7.1	−5.9	—	−1.7	−9.5	−5.9
Abortion	−2.8	−4.3	−3.7	−3.9	−3.1	−5.1	−4.5	−4.0
Others	12.0	−4.0	—	—	11.0	−3.8	—	—
Due to marital composition	−5.0	−7.3	−5.8	−3.1	−3.9	−6.3	−3.7	−3.5
Age at marriage	−7.7	−8.8	−4.7	−4.7	−6.9	−7.6	−4.2	−3.7
Widowhood and divorce	2.7	1.5	−1.1	1.6	3.0	1.3	0.5	0.2
Due to age-sex composition	−1.6	−2.1	−0.3	4.1				

Note: The rates of changes presented here are calculated using the crude birth rate or total fertility rate at the beginning of each internal as denominator. Because of adjustments the total changes do not agree with those implied by table 4-8.

Source: Tai Hwan Kwon, "The Historical Background to Korea's Demographic Transition," in Robert Repetto, Kwan Tai Hwan, Kim Son Ung, Peter Donaldson, and Kim Dae Young, Economic Development, Population Policy, and the Demographic Transition in the Republic of Korea (Cambridge, Mass., Harvard Institute of International Development, 1978).

countries, fertility has fallen as rapidly for specific subgroups, but what has been unique in the Korean experience has been the breadth of the transition. It began almost simultaneously in all regions and among all classes. From 1960 onward, the fertility transition has been general.

Another kind of decomposition analysis, carried out for the period 1966–70, adequately demonstrates the change within high-fertility sub-populations. This analysis indicates that no more than 47 percent of the overall fertility change can be associated with changes in the educational and residence composition of the population (Retherford and Ogawa, 1976). The rest of the decline is associated with reductions in marital fertility *within* residence, education, and age groups. This reflects the convergence described above.

It would be desirable to present similar data for other developing countries in order to establish whether this rapid convergence in Korea has parallels elsewhere. Unfortunately, there is a surprising lack of adequate historical series regarding the evolution of fertility differentials in developing countries. A recent study indicates that Taiwan's experience resembles that of Korea: that is, a rapid convergence of fertility differentials by residence and socioeconomic status within a decade from the onset of rapid fertility decline (Freedman and coauthors, 1977). By contrast, available information for Argentina, Brazil, Peru, the Philippines, and West Malaysia—countries with much more socioeconomic stratification —indicates nonconvergence in fertility differentials over a comparable period of time.

It is reasonable to speculate that the rapid convergence of fertility differentials in Korea is attributable to the degree of social and economic equality and integration which have been preserved. The high degree of cultural homogeneity and an absence of strong class barriers implies little resistance to the diffusion of low-fertility values or to the spread of contraceptive practice. Highly stratified countries can generate an urban, educated elite with low fertility, but with little diffusion to the rest of the population, so that overall fertility remains high. In countries like Korea and Taiwan, which are characterized by cultural homogeneity and a relative lack of socioeconomic stratification, diffusion has been extremely rapid. This rapid diffusion was characteristic of changes in family-size norms, marriage patterns, and birth-control practices.

Changes in Marriage Patterns and Desired Family Size. Family-size values seemed to maintain considerable stability during the decade

Table 4-8.   The Ideal Number of Children, by Age and Education of Women, for Korea, for Selected Years

Year and age of women	All levels of education			Level of education			
	Urban	Rural	National	No school	Primary	Middle	High and above
1965							
20–29	3.3	3.9	3.7	4.0	3.7	3.3	3.0
30–39	3.7	4.2	4.1	4.3	3.9	3.6	3.3
1966							
20–29	3.3	3.9	3.7	4.0	3.7	3.3	3.2
30–39	3.6	4.2	4.0	4.3	4.0	3.5	3.3
1967							
20–29	3.3	3.9	3.7	4.0	3.7	3.3	3.1
30–39	3.6	4.1	4.0	4.2	3.9	3.5	3.3
1971							
20–29	3.2	3.6	3.4	3.9	3.5	3.1	3.1
30–39	3.4	4.1	3.8	4.1	3.9	3.4	3.2
1973							
20–29	2.8	3.2	2.9	3.2	3.2	2.9	2.6
30–39	2.9	3.5	3.2	3.7	3.3	2.9	2.6
1974							
<25	2.6	2.9	2.7	3.1	2.8	2.7	2.3
25–34	2.8	3.2	3.2	3.4	3.1	2.8	2.5
35–44	3.2	3.6	3.5	3.6	3.4	3.1	3.0
All	3.2	3.6	3.5	3.6	3.4	3.1	3.0

Source: John Ross, "Transition to the Small Family, A Comparison of 1964–73 Time Trends in Korea and Taiwan" (New York, Center for Population and Family Health, Columbia University, 1976).

of the 1960s, even though actual fertility was rapidly declining. This is not paradoxical: the decline stemmed from the delay in family formation and the reduction in excess fertility at later childbearing ages. Only in the 1970s has there been rapid movement toward a small family norm of two or three children, as is shown in table 4-8.

Table 4-8 also demonstrates the pervasiveness of this change in values. Between 1965–74, desired family size declined as rapidly, and perhaps more rapidly for young women in rural areas than for those in urban areas. The same is true for differentials based on educational classes: the planned fertility of women with no schooling fell at least as rapidly as those of women with high-school and university educations.

A more sensitive indicator (see table 4-9)—the percentage of women at various parities wanting no more children—displays greater change.

Table 4-9. Percentage of Married Women in Korea Who Want No More Children, Classified by Number of Living Children and Living Sons, for 1965, 1971, and 1973

Total living children	No. of living sons	Women wanting no more children (%)		
		1965	1971	1973
0	0	11	6	5
1	0	4	6	4
	1	14	11	14
2	0	0	9	12
	1	22	32	36
	2	44	47	61
3	0	9	11	31
	1	34	45	60
	2+	66	79	85
4	0	12	29	N.A.
	1	41	48	65
	2+	87	88	92
5+	0	20	21	N.A.
	1	50	63	67
	2+	97	96	97

Note: N.A., not available.
Source: John Ross, "Transition to the Small Family, A Comparison of 1964–1973 Time Trends in Korea and Taiwan" (New York, Columbia University Center for Population and Family Health, 1976).

Many more women with two children are willing to stop childbearing after one son; many more women with three or four children are willing to stop childbearing even without having a son. This suggests some weakening of the traditional preference for sons under the weight of the growing consensus favoring small families. It also reflects the children's improved survival probabilities. The infant mortality rate has fallen from about 140 per 1,000 in 1954–60 to 85 in 1965–70, and to 50 in 1975 (U.S. Bureau of the Census, 1978).

Table 4-10 demonstrates similar trends for age at marriage, which has changed to as great an extent in rural areas and among less-educated women as it has among urban and educated women. This is somewhat understandable, in that many of the socioeconomic changes affecting age at marriage cut across these categories: the disruptions of the wartime period, the temporary shortage of eligible husbands following the restora-

Table 4-10.   Mean Age at First Marriage, Classified by Year of Occurrence and
Education of Wife

Year of occurrence	All levels of education	Schooling				
		None	Primary	Middle	High	College
1944–49	17.7	16.7	17.3	N.A.	N.A.	N.A.
1950–54	19.2	18.8	19.0	18.9	20.4	N.A.
1955–59	20.4	20.1	20.3	20.9	21.5	N.A.
1960–64	21.7	21.1	21.1	22.1	23.5	23.5
1965–69	22.4	22.3	21.5	22.5	23.4	24.5
1970–73	22.8	N.A.	22.3	22.5	23.9	24.3

Note: N.A., not available.
Source: Kun Yom Song and Seung Hyan Han, *National Family Planning and Fertility
Survey: A Comprehensive Report* (Seoul, Korean Institute for Family Planning, 1974)
p. 223.

tion of peace; the greater urbanization and nuclearization of households;
the prevalence of migration, and the difficulties facing young men in se-
curing employment and establishing a household; the requirements of
military service; and the rapid increase in employment opportunities for
unmarried women. Moreover, the number of those married at young ages
had fallen in urban areas to such an extent that during the 1970s improved
economic circumstances had permitted some relaxation, and even a small
reversal in the rapid decline. This contributed substantially to the convergence, since age at marriage continued its rise in rural areas (Lee,
Chang, and Yu, 1975).

Changes in Contraceptive Practice.   Contraception had little to do
with the early fall in fertility. As late as 1964, well after the onset of rapid
fertility decline, only 12 percent of women of reproductive age reported
ever having used contraceptives. By 1973, this figure had grown to 55
percent, and among older married women, especially those in urban areas,
over three-quarters had ever used contraceptives. This is an extremely
rapid diffusion; one which, if anything, seems to have accelerated in the
early 1970s. Moreover, it is one which penetrated all strata of Korean
society. By 1973 differences in contraceptive experience between urban
and rural residents, and between more- and less-educated women, had
virtually disappeared. There was particularly rapid growth of experience
among less-educated women: the proportions of women with no schooling who reported they had used contraceptives rose from 5 percent to
53 percent during 1964–73, while the proportion of women with high-

school educations or more who had ever practiced contraception rose from 52 percent to 62 percent (Song and Han, 1974).

Of more relevance is the percentage of women currently using contraception. As table 4-11 demonstrates, this has also increased dramatically, and differentials by educational status and residence also substantially declined.

There are still substantial differentials by education in the timing of the first use of contraception. In 1973, on the average, women with no schooling had been married for thirteen years before they first used contraceptives; women with college educations had been married for only four (Song and Han, 1974, page 117). Even controlling for age, education is an important factor in distinguishing early from late practitioners of family-planning methods (Lee and Lee, 1973). Educated couples are substantially less likely to profess the desire for no additional children, and yet be unprotected by contraception (Freedman and Coombs, 1974, pages 62–63).

Paralleling the changes in family-size values, it is not only parity that is the critical determining factor in current use, but especially the number of living sons. At any parity, the use of contraceptives is strongly associated with the number of males among the children (Lee and Lee, 1973, page 27). The greater willingness of women to limit births after having borne only one son, or even no son, is part of a trend toward adoption of contraception early in marriage, at younger ages, and at lower parities. More women are apparently attempting to space their children; and many more women are intervening before their fertility exceeds that which they consider ideal.

Korean women have proved themselves both determined and innovative in their desire to control births. Reliance on the intrauterine device (IUD) which, under the impetus of the family-planning program, accounted for one-half of all current use in 1966, has declined, except among older, high-parity rural women; and the use of the oral pill, conventional methods, and sterilization has greatly increased. Although first-method continuation rates for the IUD and other methods are low and have declined over time, extended use-effectiveness for all methods and the percentages of women not giving birth following adoption of one method are a great deal higher. This reflects both the adoption of other methods when one proves unsatisfactory, and recourse to abortion in the event of contraceptive failure. The totality of all methods together has been quite effective. Some indication of this is available in the data pre-

Table 4-11. Percentage of Married Women Currently Using Contraception in Korea, by Selected Characteristics and Years

Characteristic	1964	1965	1967	1971	1973	1974[a]	1976
Percentage of women currently using contraception	9.0	16.4	20.2	24.6	34.5	32.6	43.9
Total number	4,008	3,442	3,623	4,549	2,028	5,420	5,014
Age							
20–24	4.4	5.7	4.0	6.9	12.9	13.4	15.9
25–29	9.8	12.7	14.2	15.5	27.4	28.0	31.7
30–34	13.2	23.6	26.9	27.4	36.4	44.0	55.5
35–39	13.9	24.1	33.1	38.0	49.8	50.8	61.2
40–44	5.8	10.4	16.3	26.8	33.7	33.6	44.8
45–49	1.9	N.A.	N.A.	N.A.	N.A.	10.7	N.A.
Parity							
0	N.A.	(5.5)	(.9)[b]	(3.0)	3.4	7.1[c]	4.6
1	N.A.	4.3	2.4	5.9	14.6	10.9	17.9
2	N.A.	12.2	11.9	20.2	33.2	36.7	43.9
3	N.A.	14.9	22.2	28.7	49.1	43.4	56.2
4	N.A.	20.3	29.9	31.9	44.2	43.4	59.0
5 or more	N.A.	23.2	30.6	31.6	41.8	33.2	48.8
Residence							
Urban	N.A.	21.4	26.0	27.4	36.5	35.6	47.6
Rural	N.A.	14.0	17.3	22.7	32.7	29.3	39.8
Education							
None	4.6[d]	9.8	18.7	20.9	27.5	25.2	37.2
Literate	N.A.	15.9	18.4	24.6	33.8	N.A.	45.5
Primary school	13.8	15.8	21.7	24.5	35.2	32.0	42.4
Middle school	35.5	30.8	25.7	32.4	42.9	35.2	44.2
High school or more	N.A.	33.5	36.4	39.5	47.8	42.6	50.6

Note: N.A., not available.

Source: Published and unpublished tabulations from fertility and family planning KAP surveys conducted by the Korean Institute for Family Planning. Peter Donaldson, "The Evolution of the Korean Family-Planning Program," in Robert Repetto, Kim Dae Young, Kuan Tae Hwan, Peter Donaldson, and Son Ung Kim, *Economic Development, Population Policy, and the Demographic Transition in the Republic of Korea* (Cambridge, Mass., 1978).

[a] Data for 1974 are based on ever-married, nonpregnant women and thus are somewhat lower than corresponding data for all currently married women.

[b] Figures in parentheses are based on too few cases to be reliable.

[c] Data refer to living children, not parity.

[d] Data refer to ever-use which includes both past and current users.

Table 4-12.   Age-Specific Marital Fertility Rates for Fecund Women in Korea, by
Age and Birth Limitation Practice, 1970

Age	Fecund women	Nonusers	Contraception only	Contraception and abortion	Abortion only
15–24	388	407	143	217	238
25–29	361	409	481	154	188
30–24	232	325	80	53	82
35–39	136	243	39	75	88
40–49	64	109	4	49	37
Total fertility rate	5,905	6,456	3,735	2,740	3,165
Index: nonusers equal 1.00	.79	1.00	.50	.37	.42

Source: Kun Yom Song, "Birth Averted by Family Planning in Korea, 1960–70"
(Seoul, Korean Institute for Family Planning, 1973).

sented in table 4-12, based on the 1971 Fertility-Abortion Survey. Table
4-12 compares the age-specific rates of nonusers with those who have
reported various combinations of birth-control methods. The total fertility rate of the group using contraception and abortion is less than 40
percent of the rate for nonusers, and, for a synthetic cohort, implies a
complete family size of fewer than three children. Effective fertility regulation has become characteristic, not of an educated elite, but of a growing majority of Korean women.

Changes in the Control of Fertility Through Abortion.   Prior to the
diffusion of effective means of contraception, abortion was the most
important means of birth control among married Korean women. Even
though technically illegal until 1973, abortions have been readily available at a relatively low cost, at least to urban women (Hong, 1974, page
369).

Even in 1961, at the beginning of the fertility decline and the first
year for which any data are available, there was apparently one induced
abortion for every nine live births. Since then, abortion became rapidly
more widespread until the early 1970s, at which point the abortion rate
seems to have leveled off or declined in cities, while continuing to increase
in rural areas (table 4-13). Abortion rates are extremely high among
older women, especially among those aged thirty-five to thirty-nine. These
rates imply that among older women, at least in urban areas, induced

Table 4-13.   Age-Specific Marital Abortion Rates by Residence for Selected Years in Korea

Residence and age	1961	1963	1966	1971	1973
National					
20–24	24	16	15	46	86
25–29	27	29	56	69	75
30–34	49	58	75	128	137
35–39	31	40	87	119	88
40–44	10	—	44	37	22
Total national abortion rate	705	715	1,385	1,995	2,055
Urban					
20–24	N.A.[a]	29	31	76	29
25–29	N.A.	43	101	105	78
30–34	N.A.	93	123	160	132
35–39	N.A.	65	132	161	140
40–44	N.A.	—	51	39	46
Total urban abortion rate		1,150	2,190	2,705	2,160
Rural					
20–24	N.A.	6	—	21	139
25–29	N.A.	18	15	21	72
30–34	N.A.	33	44	99	142
35–39	N.A.	22	51	91	49
40–44	N.A.	—	39	36	5
Total rural abortion rate		395	745	1,340	2,035

Note: N.A., not available.
Source: Kun Yong Song and Seung Hyan Han, *National Family Planning and Fertility Survey: A Comprehensive Report* (Seoul, Korean Institute for Family Planning, 1974).

abortions outnumber live births. In fact, in Seoul in 1971, the year the urban abortion rate peaked, there were two abortions per live birth among women in this age group; in other urban areas during the same year there were 1.5 abortions (Watson and Hong, 1976, page 43).

Differentials in experience with abortion have been narrowing, not only by age and residence, but also by the educational status of the women. Partly, but not entirely, because of its urban bias, abortion has been a method of birth control more frequently used by better-educated women. In 1965, an early year for which comparable data are available, there were marked differentials by education in the use of abortion, especially among younger women. By 1973 these differentials had virtually disappeared for women between the ages of twenty and twenty-nine and were greatly reduced for women in their thirties.

Table 4-14. Characteristics of Wives with Abortion Experience and of All Currently Married Women in Korea, 1971

Duration of marriage and wife's education	No. of pregnancies		No. of live births	
	Aborters	All wives	Aborters	All wives
Total	6.7	4.6	4.0	3.6
Duration of marriage (yr)				
5	2.9	1.7	1.2	1.2
5–9	4.9	3.6	2.6	2.8
10–14	6.3	5.2	3.6	4.0
15–19	7.5	6.3	4.5	5.0
20–24	8.2	7.0	5.4	5.8
25–29	9.2	7.5	6.3	6.3
Education				
None	7.9	5.7	5.5	5.0
Primary	6.7	4.5	4.2	3.5
Middle	6.2	3.7	3.2	2.5
High school	6.1	3.8	3.0	2.3
College	5.2	3.0	2.8	1.8

Source: Walter Watson and Sung-Bong Hong, The Increasing Utilization of Induced Abortion in Korea (Seoul, Korea University Press, 1976) p. 72.

The importance of abortion as a means of preventing excess fertility among older women is clear. By 1970 one-third of all fourth pregnancies and almost one-half of all sixth pregnancies were aborted (Moon, Han, and Choi, 1973, page 89). As table 4-14 demonstrates, although for any duration of marriage, aborters had about one more pregnancy than all married women, they had, on the average, experienced fewer live births than all married women with comparable marital exposures. Table 4-14 also shows that abortion had similarly done much to eliminate the differential in births between aborters and nonaborters in all educational categories.

From this review of the mechanisms by which Korean fertility declined rapidly since 1960, there have been two important insights. The first is the finding that the speed of the transition cannot be explained by the rapid structural and compositional shifts in the population. Much is attributable to the convergence of fertility differentials, stemming from the rapid pace of fertility decline among traditionally high-fertility subgroups—the poor, the uneducated, the rural households.

The second insight is that this convergence was not just a matter of the increasing availability of contraceptives. It has sometimes been alleged that the fall in birth rates in rural areas, for example, was due to the diffusion of contraceptive practice through the efforts of the family-planning program. The facts do not support this view. The convergence of fertility differentials was due to several important changes, of which the rapid adoption of program contraceptives was only one. The others include (1) the continued fall in the proportion of young women married among rural and less-educated households, which contributed substantially to the convergence of fertility differentials; (2) the changes in desired family sizes; (3) diffusion in abortion throughout the population, especially in cases of contraceptive failure; and (4) the increased use of nonprogram sources of contraception among high-fertility groups. The demographic effects of all these changes are highly interdependent, and cannot be independently measured. However, all were important. All followed the same pattern of rapid diffusion throughout all classes of Korean families, leading to the early narrowing of socioeconomic differentials in fertility.

THE EFFECTS OF CHANGING ECONOMIC OPPORTUNITIES ON FERTILITY

The emphasis in past sections on the pervasiveness of the fertility decline, and the fact that virtually all subgroups of the population have experienced demographic change during the same periods and almost at the same rate, should not lead to underestimation of the structural changes which have brought large fractions of the population into contact with modern institutions: schools, factories, cities. At an extraordinary rate, Koreans have been drawn off the farms into nontraditional ways of living and working.

Since 1963 the real GNP has grown at an average rate of over 11 percent per year. This sustained growth, in which most groups have shared, has meant substantial expansion in perceived and actual opportunities.

Alternative Sources of Economic Security.   In traditional Korean society, parents could expect from their children and their families obedience, loyalty, care, labor services, support in case of need, and a home in later years. For the traditional head of household, who was typically a marginal farmer on a rented holding, there were very substantial benefits from a large family, since the flow of services tended to be from the younger to the older generation. At the same time, there were few alternative means by which the household could cushion itself against the insecurities of life. Accumulation of valuable assets as a hedge against the future was difficult: land was closely held, incomes were low, and savings opportunities minimal. Jobs or occupations which could be called secure were rare. Institutional forms of insurance or protection against calamities were nonexistent.

The postwar years have witnessed dramatic changes in these conditions. The flow of resources from younger to older generations has been greatly reduced, if not reversed. Increasing school enrollment has reduced the participation rate of young male workers from over 60 percent for males between the ages of fifteen and nineteen in 1960 to 42 percent in 1974, and has raised the cost of child-rearing. The decline of the family enterprise, the migration of young people to the cities, and the growing nucleation of household residence patterns has reduced the labor and financial payment which the younger generation provides to their elders. Paralleling this change in the net economic value of children to their parents, there has been a gradual shift in attitudes. The Korean family is rapidly becoming child-centered, along Western lines, rather than parent-centered, the traditional orientation.

Also, there have emerged much more substantial opportunities for households to provide for themselves in other ways. Savings, the accumulation of secure assets, and participation in institutionalized pension and insurance schemes, have brought a greater degree of security to the large majority of Korean families. Between 1953–55 and 1972–74, the current flow of real household savings per capita has approximately tripled. Throughout most of the period of rapid development, a relatively favorable climate has been established for the accumulation of assets by households; the inflation rate has been kept within moderate limits; and real interest rates have been positive in all but a few years, and generally quite high, averaging 4.5 percent, during the period 1957–75.

The widespread ownership and rapidly increasing value of real property in Korea has been a source of rapidly increasing wealth for private households. In rural areas, the postwar land reform converted over 90 percent of farm households into proprietors. Since 1957, the average price of arable land has increased in real terms by something between one-third and one-half. In urban areas, due to the rapid pace of growth and the limited supplies of usable land, the increase in values has been much more dramatic. In real terms, the rise was equivalent to an

Table 4-15. Major Social Insurance Programs in Korea, 1974–75

Program	Year adopted	Coverage (1000s)	Risks covered
Civil servants pensions	1960	456	Old age, disability, maternity, death, sickness, and illness
Military pensions	1963	119	Old age, disability, death, sickness, and maternity
Industrial accidents compensation	1963	1,222	Medical and cash benefits
Medical insurance	1963	9	Sickness and maternity
Private school teachers pension	1973	45	Old age, disability, death, sickness, and maternity
National welfare pensions	1973	1,000	Old age, disability, and death

Source: Chong Kee Park, Social Security in Korea (Seoul, Korean Development Institute, 1976).

average annual rate of increase of seventeen percent. Since a large and increasing fraction of urban households live in their own houses, this increase has provided widespread capital gains.

The rapid growth of a variety of forms of institutional savings reinforces this conclusion. The number of life insurance policies in force grew from 1.2 million in 1964 to 3.7 million in 1972. If this is related to the 5.8 million households in Korea in 1970 and the 2.5 million urban households, it is apparent that the majority of households are now covered.

Other forms of social insurance are available for substantial numbers of households, at least in the nonagricultural sector. Table 4-15 summarizes these programs which cover, in the aggregate, 2.8 million persons. If it is assumed that they protect the main earner of the household, by and large, then they probably extend to a majority of households outside the agricultural sector. In the agricultural sector, institutional protection is considerably less.

In general, the economic growth of the postwar period has brought with it a decline in the value of children as sources of economic security, and at the same time an increasing number of alternatives have become available, in the form of increasing real property, financial wealth, and participation in insurance and social security programs, to a majority of Korean households. These developments have weakened the motivation for larger families.

Educational Development. Among the new opportunities open to Korean households as a consequence of socioeconomic development, none has been more highly valued or eagerly grasped than access to education. Investments in education have averaged 9 percent of the GNP over the period 1960–74, and approximately two-thirds of this represents direct investment by households. Consequently, the educational status of the adult population and school-enrollment rates have changed dramatically.

These changes represent a two-edged sword with respect to fertility. On the one side, the rise in the educational status of the adult population has contributed substantially to the preservation of socioeconomic equality. This rise, especially within the female population, has been seen to be closely associated with the decrease in fertility and its components. Despite the rapid convergence of fertility differentials, available multivariate analysis still shows education of the woman to be the factor most closely associated with remaining differences in fertility levels. On the other side, rising school-enrollment rates have represented a substantial increase in the costs of child-rearing, and have been important in the spread of small-family norms.

The extent of differentials in cumulative fertility by education are depicted in table 4-16, which contains unpublished data from the 1974 Korean National Fertility Survey (see also page 110). Other tabulations from the 1974 survey, not reproduced here, indicate that educational differentials persist when background variables other than residence are held constant, such as household income, education of husband, and the family's religion.

Accordingly, table 4-17 shows the rapid replacement of unschooled birth cohorts with better educated ones over the period 1944–74. This stems from the abrupt change from the preindependence system of narrow, elitist educational entry to the postwar implementation of universal compulsory education.

This development is in itself sufficient to "explain" a sizable part of the total drop in fertility. While precise measures are not available, the decomposition analysis by Retherford and Ogawa (1976) suggests that perhaps 25 percent of the drop between 1966–70 might be attributable to changes in the educational composition of the female population. For the period 1960–66, the contribution would have been higher, because educational differentials were then higher, and more rapid compositional changes were taking place.

Table 4-16. Mean Number of Children Ever Born in Korea, According to Wife's Education, Residence, and Duration of Marriage

| | | Place of residence | | |
| | | Rural | | |
Wife's education and literacy	Urban	Townships	Villages	All
All women				
No school, does not read	4.6	5.5	5.8	5.5
No school, does read	4.0	5.6	5.3	4.9
Primary dropout, does not read	4.1	5.5	4.9	4.7
Primary dropout, does read	4.0	4.4	4.7	4.4
Primary graduate	3.2	3.4	3.5	3.3
Middle school	2.2	2.6	2.2	2.2
High school	2.4	2.0	2.6	2.4
College or higher	2.2	2.0	2.7	2.3
Women less than 10 yr since first marriage				
No school, does not read	2.5	1.9	2.8	2.5
No school does read	2.5	1.0	2.1	2.3
Primary dropout, does not read	2.5	4.0	2.4	2.5
Primary dropout, does read	2.0	2.3	2.2	2.1
Primary graduate	2.0	2.0	1.9	2.0
Middle school	1.7	1.7	1.6	1.7
High school	1.5	1.7	1.6	1.6
College or higher	1.6	3.0	1.7	1.6
Women 10–20 yr since first marriage				
No school, does not read	3.9	4.7	4.8	4.6
No school, does read	4.3	5.4	4.8	4.7
Primary dropout, does not read	4.1	5.0	4.8	4.6
Primary dropout, does read	3.8	4.7	4.7	4.4
Primary graduate	3.8	3.9	4.4	4.1
Middle school	3.3	4.1	3.6	3.4
High school	3.2	3.2	3.6	3.2
College or higher	2.8	0.0	3.6	2.8
Women 20 yr or more since first marriage				
No school, does not read	5.1	6.5	6.6	6.2
No school, does read	4.6	6.1	5.9	5.6
Primary dropout, does not read	4.7	5.9	6.0	5.6
Primary dropout, does read	5.2	5.7	6.1	5.7
Primary graduate	4.8	5.5	5.7	5.2
Middle school	4.5	3.7	4.7	4.5
High school	4.2	3.0	5.1	4.4
College or higher	3.8	1.0	4.3	3.7

Source: Republic of Korea, Bureau of Statistics, Economic Planning Board, 1974 National Fertility Survey.

Table 4-17. The Percentage of Korean Population, Ages Fourteen and Older, by Years of Education, for Selected Years

Year	Sex	No edu-cation	1–6 yr	7–9 yr	10–12 yr	13–14 yr	13 yr and older	15 yr and older	Un-known no. of yr
1944[a]	Total	86.6	11.3[b]		1.8	0.2		0.1	
	Male	78.2	18.4[b]		3.0	0.3		0.1	
	Female	94.8	4.5		0.6	0.1		0.0	
1960	Total	43.7	36.0	9.6	7.6	1.2		1.4	0.5
	Male	31.8	37.8	13.7	11.8	2.0		2.5	0.4
	Female	55.1	34.3	5.7	3.7	0.4		0.3	0.5
1966	Total	30.8	40.0	11.1	13.6	1.2		3.3	
	Male	21.5	37.7	13.8	19.4	2.1		5.5	
	Female	39.8	42.2	8.4	8.0	0.4		1.2	
1970	Total	23.5	39.3	17.9	13.8	1.9		3.6	
	Male	15.8	34.9	21.6	18.8	3.0		5.9	
	Female	30.9	43.5	14.4	9.0	0.8		1.4	
1974[c]	Total	20.3	36.0	20.8	17.2	N.A.	5.7	N.A.	
	Male	13.6	31.7	23.7	22.0	N.A.	9.0	N.A.	
	Female	26.5	39.9	18.0	12.6	N.A.	2.6	N.A.	

Source: Noel F. McGinn, Donald R. Snodgrass, Yong Bong Kim, Shin Bok Kim, Quee Yong Kim, *Education and Development in Korea*, Harvard East Asian Monograph no. 90 (Cambridge, Mass., Council on East Asian Studies, Harvard University, 1977).

[a] The figures for 1944 include population, ages fifteen and older, for the whole of Korea.

[b] Includes secondary school dropouts (seven to eleven years).

[c] For 1974, the age breakdown available is "13 yr and older," not "13–14 yr" and "15 yr and older" as given for previous years.

Moreover, educational development has had a substantial effect on the ages at which women marry. Among the factors impinging on female age at marriage excluding those affecting men, educational attainment has had the strongest effect (Kim, Rider, Harper, and Yang, 1974). Education for women has widened employment opportunities outside of the agricultural sector and family enterprises. Also, educated women are less willing to accept the traditional subordinate role within the household. In particular, they are usually quite reluctant to move in with their in-laws and accept the position of virtual servants to their mothers-in-law, who would tend to be less educated than themselves and to hold old-fashioned attitudes. They would prefer to delay marriage until a separate household could be established, and to work and save toward that goal (Park, 1973).

Enrollment rates increased gradually in the colonial period, but spurted after 1944, when educational opportunities were markedly broadened. By the start of the Korean War, the primary school enrollment rate was 84 percent of the relevant age group, and since 1960 it has been effectively 100 percent for both boys and girls. Government support for education in Korea has been concentrated on primary schooling, which has absorbed over 80 percent of public spending on education. On average over the years, the government has provided 80 percent to 90 percent of the total in-school costs at primary level.

Strong social demand has also pushed up enrollment rates at secondary and higher levels, and government policy here has contributed to the preservation of socioeconomic equity in other ways. Entry into postprimary education is not markedly differentiated according to class background by international standards. This is because of (1) the broad base of primary education from which students are drawn; (2) reliance on a strict examination system to ration entry to higher education, and, until recently, to secondary schools also; and (3) the widely shared appreciation of education as the key to socioeconomic advancement, and the willingness of parents to incur heavy financial burdens in order to provide their children this opportunity. Yet, inevitably, there is a positive relationship between the class background of a child and his or her chances of entering successively higher schooling levels. Therefore, the government policy of forcing households to bear a preponderant share of postprimary educational expenses has contributed to equality by avoiding a potential subsidy to the relatively well-to-do. In 1973, for example, the percentage shares of government spending in total in-school costs were 12 percent, 22 percent, and 24 percent for middle schools, high schools, and colleges, respectively. Since there are substantial out-of-school costs altogether by households, the public share in total costs has been even less.

Private contributions have been elicited only partially through fees. In addition, except for primary schools, the government has made no attempt to keep up with the growth of demand by increasing the number of available places. As a result, while enrollment in nongovernmental schools accounted for only 1 percent of total primary enrollment in 1973, it accounted for 42 percent, 57 percent, and 73 percent at middle, upper secondary, and tertiary levels, respectively.

In the face of this restrictive policy, enrollment in postprimary schools has expanded since the Korean War at an average rate of 7 to 8 percent per year. For all secondary education, the enrollment ratio in

1950 was 16 percent. By 1960, it had risen to 36 percent for middle school and 24 percent for high school. By 1974 these figures were 67 percent and 37 percent, respectively, and the male–female sex ratio in secondary schools had fallen from 4:1 to 1.5:1. In colleges and universities, the enrollment rate has grown from 6 to 10 percent between 1960–74. Among countries at Korea's level of GNP per capita, all these rates are unusually high.

Behind this strong demand was the Confucian high regard for education as the pathway to social status and career advancement. This was reinforced by the experience of the immediate independence period, when educated personnel were scarce and virtually all highly trained entrants into the labor market obtained good positions and rapid advancement. The rapid growth of the modern economy permitted the absorption of young graduates. Consequently, past rates of return to educational investments seem to have been reasonably high.

From the standpoint of the parental household, however, the advancement of enrollment rates raised the investment costs of children substantially. In 1966 the student-paid expenses of middle school were 11.5 percent of the mean household disposable income; for high schools and colleges, the burdens were 18 percent and 40 percent, respectively (Kim, 1976, page 40). Since parents can hope to capture only a small part, if any, of the returns to their expenditures, these rising investment levels are experienced mainly as the costs of ensuring children good career prospects. Educational advancements have "raised the ante" in job competition, so that greater defensive investments are required in order to provide children the same prospective place in the occupational hierarchy.

As an approximation to the *ex ante* expected educational costs to parents of raising a child, an index was constructed by weighting the total student-paid costs at each level of education (in 1970 prices) by the enrollment ratio at that level. The resulting figure is the expected household cost, assuming that the child would experience the prevailing chances of enrollment at each level. The index increases both with rising enrollment ratios and with rising costs. The index is conservative for two reasons: first, out-of-school cost increases have probably been underestimated; and second, with rising enrollment rates, the cohort experience would differ substantially from the period rates. Nonetheless, with 1960 as the base, the index of expected educational costs in real terms rose by 16 percent by 1966, 43 percent by 1970, and 66 percent by 1974 (table 4-18).

Table 4-18. Changes in Expected Household Educational Expenditures in Korea, for Selected Years

Year and school level	Percentage enrolled	Costs per student per year (1970 won)	No. of yr	Total expected costs (won)	Weighted average costs (won)	Index of expected costs (1960=100)
1960						
Primary	96	7,819	0	45,037		
Middle	36	31,255	3	33,755		
High	24	49,433	3	35,592		
Above	6.0	109,674	4	26,322	140,706	100
1966						
Primary	100	7,819	6	46,914		
Middle	47	31,255	3	44,070		
High	27	49,433	3	40,041		
Above	7.2	109,674	4	31,588	162,611	116
1970						
Primary	100	8,769	6	52,614		
Middle	51	36,365	3	55,638		
High	28	53,159	3	44,654		
Above	8.5	142,978	4	48,612	201,518	143
1974						
Primary	100	8,069	6	48,414		
Middle	67	36,971	3	74,312		
High	37	48,626	3	53,975		
Above	9.6	148,220	4	56,916	233,617	166

Source: Calculated from data in Yong Bong Kim, "Education and Economic Growth," in Noel F. McGinn, Donald R. Snodgrass, Yong Bong Kim, Shin Bok Kim, and Quee Yong Kim, *Education and Development in Korea*, Harvard East Asian Monograph no. 90 (Cambridge, Mass., Council on East Asian Studies, Harvard University, 1977).

In summary, the development of education in Korea has contributed to socioeconomic equity and to lower fertility in two ways: first, by providing widespread primary education to the population which has entered reproductive ages since 1960; and second, by raising the costs to household of investments in their children's education beyond primary level.

Changes in Economic Structure.   The spearhead of Korea's rapid economic growth has been the expansion of labor-intensive manufacturing industries producing largely for exports. This development pattern has resulted in two structural shifts of major importance to the understanding of the fertility decline. The rapid absorption of labor into nontraditional employment has been the key to the rise in real wages and the preservation of a relatively equal distribution of income. At the same time, it has drawn surplus labor from the rural economy into urban industry; and has drawn women out of domestic activity into paid employment. Both urbanization and the increasing labor-force participation rate of women have been closely associated with the changes in age at marriage and in marital fertility.

Urbanization and Migration. The increases in the urban population during the periods of political and military upheaval were abrupt. Since 1960 the pace of urbanization has slackened but is nonetheless rapid. Between 1960–75 the urban population grew at an average annual rate of 6.3 percent per year. By comparison, the overall population grew at 2.2 percent per year, and the rural population declined slightly. Since 1960, in other words, the entire increase of the population, of roughly 10 million persons, contributed to the growth of cities. At the outset of the period of declining fertility, in 1960, 28 percent of the population lived in urban areas; by 1975, over half the total population did so. Over the decade, 1960–70, migration from rural areas contributed about two-thirds of the total growth of cities (Eui-Yong Yu, 1973), and there is every reason to believe that migration has since become an even more important component of overall urban growth.

The determinants of this high degree of mobility and rapid urbanization, taking place since 1960, are readily understood. Employment in secondary and tertiary sectors grew extremely rapidly over this period, while employment in agriculture remained static. In fact, employment of primary earners in agriculture declined, and total employment in this sector was maintained by the increasing participation of women as unpaid secondary workers. These differential growth rates in employment stemmed not only from the lower-income elasticity of demand for agricultural output, but primarily, from the export-oriented, manufacturing-led pattern of development. Since jobs in the industrial and service sectors are predominantly urban, while agricultural jobs are, of course, rural, workers had to move to the cities.

Other influences merely tended to reinforce the basic pattern. Until recently, rural incomes lagged behind urban incomes substantially. Also, the rapid pace of modernization, and the impetus given to the growth of the primate city by the war and postwar experience of Korea, dictated that Seoul should be the center for educational and cultural opportunities, as well as for economic and governmental activities. Furthermore, the absence of cultural and linguistic barriers to movement facilitated the movement of people to other areas in search of expanded opportunities.

The shift in the population from rural to urban residence has contributed substantially to the decline in fertility (see table 4-16). Evidence from the decomposition analysis discussed earlier suggests that the shift in population to the cities was associated with up to 25 percent of the overall decline. Multivariate analyses corroborate this. A recent analysis, based on the 1 percent household sample of the 1970 census, concludes: "According to the statistical analysis, residence background . . . is the most important variable influencing fertility. Women living in cities have fewer children, and the difference is statistically significant. Migration status is the second most important variable. For all age groups, regardless of the place of residence, migrants have fewer children than non-migrants" (Ro, 1976, page 261).

Both residence background and migrant status affect fertility rates. A study, based on the own-children method of fertility estimation and the 1970, 10 percent census sample, yielded estimates of age-specific and total fertility rates for migrants and nonmigrants in urban and rural areas for the years 1965–70. These data are presented in table 4-19. The pure residence effect can most readily be seen by reading vertically the column on the age-specific fertility rates of nonmigrants in metropolitan, urban, and rural areas.

Migrant fertility tends to be lower than nonmigrant fertility, except that rural origin or rural destination of migration results in higher fertility, in comparison with the fertility of urban and metropolitan nonmigrants. Otherwise, the fertility of migrants is lower than that of nonmigrant populations, both in the place of origin and in the place of destination. There is a remarkable consistency of these differentials in all age groups, which is a reflection of the fact that they stem not only from differences in the age at first marriage of migrant and nonmigrant women, but also from differences in marital fertility at all ages (Park and Park, 1976).

One would expect, since migration is selective for education as well as for age, and because the basal education levels of the rural, urban, and metropolitan populations from which migrants are drawn also differ, that the introduction of controls on education would result in a modification of these findings. This is only partially true. Within all residence groups and

Table 4-19. Age-Specific and Total Fertility Rates in Korea, by Residence and Migrant Status, 1965–70

Age	Metropolitan nonmigrants	Metropolitan migrants to		
		Metropolitan areas	Urban areas	Rural areas
15–19	1.1	1.2	3.1	6.8
20–24	48.4	35.6	57.7	78.9
25–29	214.4	182.1	181.1	201.0
30–34	203.8	181.7	197.2	202.9
35–39	92.0	80.2	107.4	121.8
40–44	35.0	22.8	36.2	48.9
45–49	11.6	9.9	11.2	16.0
All	3,031.5	2,597.5	2,972.0	3,381.5

Age	Urban nonmigrants	Urban migrants to		
		Metropolitan areas	Urban areas	Rural areas
15–19	1.2	1.3	2.0	10.0
20–24	51.9	37.2	56.8	81.5
25–29	244.5	178.0	208.4	224.7
30–34	227.6	186.2	224.5	230.4
35–39	120.0	88.1	121.9	138.6
40–44	55.9	28.1	52.0	75.6
45–49	18.1	13.6	18.3	26.2
All	3,598.0	2,662.5	3,419.5	3,936.0

Age	Rural nonmigrants	Rural migrants to		
		Metropolitan areas	Urban areas	Rural areas
15–19	3.5	0.8	1.5	9.0
20–24	100.0	44.3	68.7	109.7
25–29	311.7	221.4	245.0	254.5
30–34	278.3	205.9	231.7	247.9
35–39	189.2	104.9	126.4	107.8
40–44	107.8	46.0	63.2	28.7
45–49	35.5	12.7	18.1	33.2
All	5,133.0	2,179.5	3,773.0	4,254.0

Source: J. H. Park and I. H. Park, "Migration and Female Labor Force Impact on Korean Fertility," in *The Dynamics of Migration* (Washington, D.C., Smithsonian Institution, 1976).

at any level of education, the fertility of migrants is typically lower than that of nonmigrants. The *lower* the educational status of the women, the greater are these differences.

A study of migrant and nonmigrant populations in Seoul has shown that in-migrant households are very likely to be nuclear in form, without older relatives to assist in the domestic work. Typically they move about in the city one or more times after their arrival in search of adequate housing: the average length of stay in the first urban residence is only one year (Yoon, 1975, page 177). In urban areas there is a severe housing scarcity. In 1970, 43 percent of urban households were without a separate dwelling, and in Seoul the percentage rose to 46 percent. On the average there were 2.7 persons per room in urban dwellings in Korea in 1970 (Mills and Song, 1979, page 3). In-migrants initially experience considerable financial difficulty. Male household heads tend to be younger and less-well educated than their city counterparts, and they are much more likely to find themselves initially in relatively low-paying blue-collar jobs. The predominant occupational shift associated with migration is from farming to urban production work. The mobility and economic pressure which accompanies migration to the city may be part of the explanation of the lower fertility rate, especially since it seems more pronounced among families at the lower end of the socioeconomic scale.

Changes in Female Work Participation.   The influx of women into the labor force has been especially rapid during the period 1960–74. Their participation rate rose from 19 percent to 30 percent in urban areas, and from 27 percent to 52 percent in rural areas. The biggest increases were experienced by young unmarried women under the age of twenty-four; the lowest by women in the child-rearing years of thirty to thirty-nine, the age bracket in which almost all are married (Kim, 1976, page 45).

The influx was accompanied by substantial changes in the occupational distribution for women workers. A rapidly rising proportion of women were engaged in production and manufacturing activities, and in office clerical jobs. A decreasing proportion were employed in agriculture. However, these changes were not nearly as dramatic as those affecting men. In 1974, 57 percent of women workers were still in agriculture, as compared with only 44 percent of men. There has also been a trend toward regular employment in organized enterprises, and away from family labor and self-employment. This has affected both men and women. The percentage of employees has risen from 22 percent to 41 percent over the period 1960–74.

The rapid rise in employment of women, especially in manufacturing, has been one by-product of the labor-intensive, export-oriented development strategy adopted in Korea. Under competitive pressure to export, manufacturers, especially in textile and other light industries, have employed low-wage, easily managed women workers.

Participation in the modern economy of factory and office has been open primarily to unmarried women, however. Eighty-four percent of economically active single women work in production, clerical, or service jobs, contrasted with only 28 percent of active married women. Forty-three percent of working married women are in agriculture, and another 24 percent in sales, usually of the small-scale family variety. Correspondingly, single women are far more likely to be regular employees; while married women tend to be unpaid family workers or self-employed. These differences are reflected in relative earnings. Those of married women, controlling for age and education, tend to be lower, but not because they systematically earn less within given occupations. Rather, they are clustered in relatively low-paid occupations or are employed as family workers.

There have been several recent investigations of the factors influencing female work participation. Demand forces have been found to predominate, especially in urban areas. At almost all age levels, an index of the demand for female labor and a measure of the unemployment rate, indicating the slackness in the labor market, have been found to be significant determinants of female labor-force participation (Kim, 1976).

Supply considerations other than marriage seem to have been relatively unimportant. There is a strong tendency for women to drop out of the labor market once they are married, even before the birth of a child. As table 4-20 indicates, this is true in urban and rural areas, as well as in the industrial and nonindustrial sectors. Participation rates are rather insensitive to the number of children in the family, which suggests that it is marriage itself which makes the difference.

In urban areas, there is a mild inverse association between work participation and the availability of other family incomes, although there is a closer relation between participation and the availability of an alternative earner. The educational attainment of the wife, which should be a good measure of her potential earnings, is also not closely related to

Table 4-20.   Labor-Force Participation Rates of Ever-Married Korean
Women, by Number of Children Ever Born, 1970

Marital status	No. of children	All Korea	Urban	Rural
All sectors				
Single		44.8	43.9	46.0
Married	0	28.3	19.6	40.0
	1	28.1	18.7	41.5
	2	30.4	19.4	45.2
	3	30.9	18.8	44.9
	4	32.2	20.4	47.6
	5	39.4	20.7	50.6
	6 or more	43.1	23.4	51.9
Nonagricultural sectors				
Single		32.0	43.0	18.0
Married	0	13.3	16.9	9.1
	1	12.0	14.8	8.9
	2	10.9	13.5	7.3
	3	10.0	13.3	7.1
	4	9.7	14.3	6.7
	5	9.2	14.6	6.3
	6 or more	7.9	14.3	5.5

Source: Unpublished tabulations from a 1 percent sample of the 1970
Korean Population and Housing Census data.

participation rates. Indeed, in Korea even professionally trained women
drop out of the labor force and become housewives when they marry.

In exploring the effects of these changes in women's work on fertility, it is useful to make the distinction between the effect on marriage
age and that on marital fertility. The former has been more significant.
In urban areas, jobs which require full-time regular attendance are competitive with marriage. Recent data from the still unpublished National
Fertility Survey of Korea, pertaining to the year 1974, indicate that the
kind of employment women engage in before marriage has been much
more important than the number of years worked in influencing their age
at marriage. There are no differences in marriage age between women employed within the family and those economically inactive before marriage,
but substantial differences exist between these groups and women employed outside the home. By contrast, the sensitivity of marriage age to
large variations in the duration of premarital work experience has been
small.

Table 4-21. Number of Children Ever Born per Ever-Married Korean Women, by Occupation (Standardized by Age), 1970

Occupation	Average no. of children ever born			No. of own children under 5 yr		
	All Korea	Urban	Rural	All Korea	Urban	Rural
Professional	3.21	2.87	3.73	0.63	0.61	0.67
Managerial	2.31	1.59	2.55	0.55	0.50	0.79
Clerical	2.30	2.24	2.67	0.45	0.43	0.51
Sales	3.80	3.63	4.07	0.71	0.65	0.81
Service	3.10	3.00	3.41	0.37	0.31	0.53
Agricultural	4.61	4.20	4.63	1.00	0.86	1.01
Production	3.90	3.32	4.37	0.69	0.48	0.87

Source: Hyo-Chai Lee and Hyoung Cho, "Fertility and Women's Labor Force Participation in Korea," in *Recent Empirical Findings on Fertility: Korea, Nigeria, Tunisia, Venezuela, Philippines,* Occasional Monograph no. 7 (Washington, D.C., International Communications Program, 1976).

Over the period 1960–74, urban jobs incompatible with marriage—such as those in production, clerical, and service industries—which are the main employers of single women, have risen from 22 percent to 35 percent of total employment of both sexes. At the same time, the share of women in these industries has increased from 23 percent of total employment to 29 percent. Over all industries, the fraction of the work force which is in paid employment, as opposed to self- or family employment, rose in the same period from 22 percent to 41 percent. These data indicate the rapid expansion in urban areas of jobs offering an alternative to marriage.

It should be kept in mind, though, that from 1960 onwards, nuptiality also declined for rural and uneducated women and those excluded from competitive career alternatives, at virtually the same pace. The lengthening of school enrollment for men, the requirement of military service, the likelihood of migration to urban areas, and the need to establish secure employment and a separate household have postponed marriage for men, and thereby for all women.

The effects on marital fertility are somewhat hard to establish since data are scarce. There are substantial differences in current fertility by occupation, as table 4-21 indicates. Using own-children under five as the measure of fertility, and with women in agriculture as the standard of comparison, one finds that the fertility level of production workers is 31 percent less, that of service workers 63 percent less, that of clerical workers 55 percent less, and so on.

Table 4-22. Mean Live Births in Korea by Age of Wife, Residence, and Employment Status, 1971

Residence	Not employed	Employment status			Total
		Self-employment	Family worker	Employee	
Seoul					
15–29	1.5	1.4	1.3	1.4	1.5
30–39	3.3	3.4	3.7	3.3	3.4
40–54	4.9	5.1	4.8	4.5	4.9
Other urban					
15–29	1.7	1.6	2.1	0.7	1.6
30–39	3.7	3.8	3.3	3.2	3.6
40–54	5.0	5.1	5.9	4.8	5.5
Rural					
15–29	2.0	2.3	2.3	1.5	2.0
30–39	4.7	4.3	4.7	4.0	4.6
40–54	6.4	5.7	6.3	6.3	6.3

Source: Hyo-Chai Lee and Hyoung Cho, "Fertility and Women's Labor Force Participation in Korea," in Recent Empirical Findings on Fertility: Korea, Nigeria, Tunisia, Venezuela, Philippines, Occasional Monograph no. 7 (Washington, D.C., International Communications Program, 1976).

These data suggest that the emergence of nontraditional employment opportunities for women has had a substantial impact on fertility rates. While this has probably been true for those women who have participated in those occupations which are associated with low birth rates, more care is required in assessing the overall impact. For one thing, there is evidence that not only is occupation related to fertility, but also to the worker's status within occupations. Women who are engaged in family enterprises are able to coordinate this with family responsibilities. It is mainly the women who are regular employees outside the household who show lower fertility (table 4-22). By and large, the fertility levels of family workers are the same as those who are not economically active.

Other factors further delimit the overall impact of these occupational changes. The percentage of women economically active and not working in the agricultural sector increased from 8.7 percent to 19.3 percent of the female labor force. It is these women who might have been affected by the employment changes which took place. However, of these, 30 percent in 1960 and 26 percent in 1974 were unpaid family workers, who show no lower fertility than the economically inactive. A further downward adjustment is required for these women. Finally, 43 percent of

Table 4-23.   Percentage of Women Affected by Occupational
and Employment Changes in Korea, 1960–74

Categories of economically active women	1960	1974
Women 15–49, and economically active	29	45
Women 15–49, and economically active and employed outside agriculture	8.7	19.3
As above, and *not* unpaid family workers	6.0	15.0
As above, and also currently married	3.4	8.6

Source: Calculated from data in Soo Kon Kim, *Labor Force
Behavior and Unemployment in Korea* (Seoul, Korea Development Institute, 1976).

the women employed outside of the agricultural sector, between the ages
of fifteen to forty-nine, were unmarried. Therefore, taking all these factors
into account, one concludes that in 1960 the *marital* fertility of only 3.4
percent of the women between the ages of fifteen to forty-nine could have
been lowered by their occupational activities, whereas in 1974 only 8.6
percent of the women were so affected. These estimates are summarized
in table 4-23. They imply that compositional changes in the female labor
force could have made only a relatively small contribution to the overall
fertility decline. An additional 5 percent of the women of reproductive
age came into jobs associated with changes within occupational and employment categories.

A MULTIVARIATE STATISTICAL MODEL APPLIED
TO RECENT FERTILITY

This section recapitulates the conclusions of the preceding historical
study, and presents the results of a multivariate statistical analysis of
recent Korean fertility which tests and quantifies those findings. Econometric modeling permits more formal tests of hypotheses, which have
been suggested by the historical material, and also allows quantitative
estimation of the socioeconomic forces acting on fertility. The results of
the analysis add another kind of evidence to that already accumulated.

The structure of the formal model, like that of the preceding historical essay, relies on the general conceptual framework proposed by
Davis and Blake (1956) in a now-classic paper. They classified the intermediate variables which determine fertility; that is, those governing sexual
union, sexual activity, risk of conception, and so forth. These are the

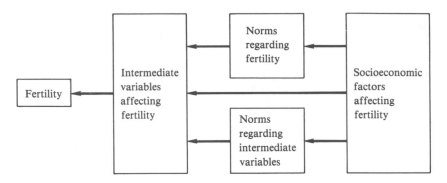

Figure 4-1. The Davis-Blake conceptual framework.

channels through which norms regarding marriage, family size, and sexual or contraceptive practice influence fertility, and hence, the channels through which socioeconomic factors affect fertility. The following schematic outline illustrates the Davis-Blake framework.

The model implied by this framework is recursive. Socioeconomic factors affect norms and the behavior of intermediate fertility variables, but not vice versa. In general, the flow of causation is uniformly from right to left. This implies that, were the model completely specified, socioeconomic factors would influence fertility only through some set of intermediate variables: for given levels of these, there would be no additional impact either of the socioeconomic variables or of norms.

For statistical estimation, a recursive model structure is convenient, because it allows the use of single-equation rather than simultaneous-equation regression techniques. Provided that error terms in the individual equations are uncorrelated, so that the variance-covariance matrix of the disturbances is diagonal, ordinary least-squares regression estimates will be not only consistent, but also unbiased with the minimum variance of all linear estimators. These conditions imply, for example, that explanatory variables omitted from any equation in the model are uncorrelated with any component of the disturbance term in any succeeding equation in the triangular model structure. Given the large number of socioeconomic factors which could be included in this analysis because of the large sample size, it is plausible that these conditions are substantially fulfilled.

In this application of the Davis-Blake framework, the intermediate variables which were taken into consideration were (1) age at first marriage and duration of marriage, and (2) contraceptive usage. Other

Table 4-24. Structure of the Recursive Econometric Fertility Model

Fertility variable	Intermediate fertility variables	Fertility-related norms	Socioeconomic variables
Children ever born alive	Age of first marriage	Preferred family size	Current age
			Child mortality experience
	Contraceptive usage	Aspirations for children's education	Length of residence and migrant status
			Rural or urban origins
		Expectations for old-age support and security	Household income per household member
			Occupation of husband
			Education of husband
			Age of marriage of husband
			Sex composition of living children
			Education of women
			Work experience of women prior to and after marriage
			Number of children of preceding generation

intermediate variables—temporary disruption of marriages, recourse to abortion, or intensity or method of contraception, for example—which have been important in the determination of the Korean birthrate could not be included. This does not compromise the recursive model structure. It does mean, however, that there will be a direct impact of socioeconomic factors and norms on fertility, even after the effects of included intermediate variables are considered.

The fertility-related norms measured for this analysis were (1) preferred family size at the time of marriage, as recounted retrospectively; (2) a measure of the parents' educational aspirations for their children; and (3) a measure of the strength of parents' expectations for economic support and old-age security from their children. To summarize, table 4-24 presents the specific model in triangular form. The last column lists

Table 4-25.   Glossary of Variables

Notation	Definition of the variable
CEB	Children ever born alive
AFM	Age of first marriage of woman, in years
DRM	Duration of marriage: Current age minus age at first marriage
PFS	Preferred family size at the time of first marriage
SCC	Number of living sons divided by number of living children
CUR	Percentage of closed birth intervals during which any contraceptive method was used
LCR	Number of years respondent has stayed in current place of residence
HIN	Average monthly household earnings per household member
HINSQ	Squared value of HIN
EPP	Years of nonfamily paid employment prior to first marriage
EPA	Years of nonfamily paid employment after first marriage
AGE	Current age of respondent in years
GUP	Dummy = 1 if respondent grew up in a rural area; zero, otherwise
MGS	Dummy = 1 if respondent has always lived in current residence
NCP	Number of children in respondent's family of origin
EAL	Index of educational aspirations for children: constructed from the expected educational attainment per child and a subjective assessment of the financial burden of educating the children
CEL	Index of expected old-age support: based on the subjective assessment by respondent of the probability of obtaining financial support from children, being able to live with them in old age, and of obtaining assistance in the event of severe difficulty.
EDL1	Dummy = 1 if respondent's educational status is none
EDL2	Dummy = 1 if respondent's educational status is primary or less
EDL3	Dummy = 1 if respondent's educational status is middle or less
EDL4	Dummy = 1 if respondent's educational status is high school or above
EDM1-4	Similar dummies for the educational status of respondent's husband
OCC1	Dummy = 1 if husband's occupation is farmer or farm laborer
OOC2	Dummy = 1 if husband's occupation is unskilled or semi-skilled laborer
OCC3	Dummy = 1 if husband's occupation is clerical, sales, or administrative
OCC4	Dummy = 1 if husband's occupation is technical, professional, or managerial worker
SPC	Child spacing: CEB divided by DRM
DCR	Experience of child mortality: the number of children still alive minus the number of children ever born alive, as a percentage of the latter (plus an infinitesimal number)

the socioeconomic factors which contribute to the explanation of norms, intermediate variables, and fertility itself.

The data for this analysis came from the 1974 Korean National Fertility Survey, Korea's contribution to the World Fertility Survey. The sample consisted of 4,570 currently married women. A glossary of variables used, and their definitions, are provided in table 4-25. The regression results are summarized in table 4-26.

The restatement of the findings of the historical essay as hypotheses begins with the conclusions regarding norms and intermediate variables, then turns to hypotheses concerning the effects of socioeconomic factors on fertility itself.

With regard to preferred family size, it was found previously that differentials by residence and education had narrowed, and that there had been a general decline in family-size norms in the period under review. These hypotheses are reflected in the regression results reported in column six. Despite the low explanatory power of the equation, as indicated by the R^2 of .19, there is a strong cohort effect; that is, young women prefer smaller families. Also, there remain educational and residential differentials; that is, women who grew up in rural areas prefer smaller families, as do women with higher educational status. The impact on achieved fertility of ideal family size at marriage is itself rather weak, once other factors are held constant.

Strong parental educational aspirations for children were found in the case study to have had a strong impact on fertility. This is confirmed by the close association of this variable in the cross-sectional analysis with fertility. After duration of marriage, educational aspirations and household income were found to be most strongly related to fertility, in terms of the standardized regression coefficients. In an earlier section, it was suggested that with rising incomes, Korean households have been eager to acquire human capital for their children. This is borne out by the regression results: educational aspirations rise sharply with household income, but then level off to a peak at approximately seven times the mean income level. These findings imply a strong substitution effect between numbers of children and superior investments in education and other assets. The effects of the parents' educational status and occupation on their educational aspirations for their children also show marked nonlinearity. Farm households tend to have much lower aspirations, and parents with middle-school educations show the most intense aspirations for their children.

With respect to the norms regarding old-age security and economic support for children, it was hypothesized that increased economic welfare and availability of institutionalized savings progressively has weakened this motivation in Korea for large families. These findings are also confirmed in the statistical analysis. These norms are weakly related to fertility, with a sign contrary to expectations. Moreover, the strength of these expectations falls rapidly with rising income levels across the sample to the upper-middle income range. Strong expectations for old-age support are typical of older parents, of households with lower or ex-

Table 4-26. Direct and Reduced-Form Estimates of Socioeconomic Factors Affecting Fertility

Explanatory variables		CEB	AFM	CUR	PFS	EAL	CEL	Reduced-form equation
		mean = 3.50	21.65	0.20	3.11	8.39	4.63	
CODE	MEAN	R^2 = 0.85	0.67	0.24	0.19	0.58	0.30	
AFM	21.65	−.101 (.49)		−.006 (−.17)				
CUR	0.20	—						
PFS	3.11	.037 (.02)		.014 (.05)				
EAL	8.39	−.313 (−.33)		−.008 (−.05)				
CEL	4.63	−.029 (−.02)		−.008 (−.04)				
DCR	[−]0.86	.520 (.06)	−.063 (−.15)		.020 (.13)			.52
AGE	34.99	.116 (.02)		—		−.116 (−.39)	.03 (.13)	.159
SCC	0.49	−.138 (−.02)		.106 (.10)		−.215 (−.03)		−.071
LCR	15.03	.008 (.05)		—			.006 (.04)	.007
HIN	1.08	−.554 (−.33)		—		.41 (.23)	−.30 (−.22)	−.673
HIN2	2.83	.034 (.20)		—		−.03 (−.19)	.02 (.13)	.043
OCC1	0.30	.261 (.05)				−.52 (−.10)	.39 (.10)	.412
OCC2	0.32	—				.35 (.07)	—	−.110
OCC3	0.23	—				.32 (.06)	—	−.100
OCC4	0.07	—				—	.25 (.04)	−.007

112

	Mean							Reduced form
EDL1	0.18	—	−2.77 (−.34)	−.170 (−.19)	.462 (.14)	—		.297
EDL2	0.50	—	−2.18 (−.35)	−.126 (−.18)	.441 (.18)	.530 (.12)		.063
EDL3	0.18	—	−1.58 (−.20)	−.092 (−.10)	.216 (.07)	1.05 (.18)		−.065
EDL4	0.10	—	−1.10 (−.11)	—	.213 (.05)	0.75 (.10)		−.051
EDM1	0.09		−2.99 (−.27)			—		.302
EDM2	0.32		−1.58 (−.24)			—		.160
EDM3	0.22		−1.00 (−.13)			.34 (.06)		−.005
EDM4	0.24		−0.32 (−.04)			.29 (.05)		−.064
EPP	2.19	—	.220 (.20)	—				−.022
EPA	6.06						.01 (.05)	−.0003
AMM	26.74		.195 (.29)					−.020
GUP	0.73				.106 (.04)			.039
NCP	6.15			—				

Note: See table 4-25 for an explanation of variables. In each column, the dependent variable is first identified, followed by its sample mean and the multiple correlation coefficient of the regression equation. In each regression, standardized regression coefficients are presented in parentheses. Regression coefficients not different from zero at the .05 confidence limit are indicated by dashes. In computing the reduced form equation presented in the last column, these coefficients were set equal to zero.

tremely high incomes, with the head of the household engaged either in farming or in managerial or professional occupations.

Regarding the intermediate fertility variables, it is obvious that the important role assigned to variations in age at marriage in the historical study is confirmed in the econometric analysis: age at first marriage is the single variable most strongly related to fertility. Moreover, the previously identified explanatory factors underlying age at marriage are also confirmed. The impact on fertility of women's work experience prior to marriage operates only through her age at marriage; that is, each year of experience, on average, raises the age at marriage by two to three months. Also, the impact of husband's and wife's education is largely through the age at marriage. The regression results also demonstrate the importance of the male's age at marriage on the woman's, as previously suggested.

The estimation of the relationship of contraceptive usage to fertility is handicapped, evidently, by the particular measure for the extent of usage adopted. The percentage of intervals between live births during which any method of contraception was used imperfectly summarizes the duration, intensity, and efficiency of use; aspects which probably require separate measures for adequate representation. The insignificance of the regression coefficient relating this variable to fertility cannot be taken to imply that contraceptive usage has not influenced Korean fertility. Moreover, the associations between this measure and fertility-related norms are mostly of an unexpected sign. On the other hand, associations with the socioeconomic factors support the hypothesis that the preference for sons and the wife's educational level have had a strong influence on when family planning is adopted.

This leads us to consider hypotheses regarding the direct and indirect effects of socioeconomic factors on fertility. First, one of the main conclusions drawn from the historical study was that the lack of sharp socioeconomic inequalities in Korea contributed to the speed of the fertility decline. The corresponding test of this, using current household data, is that the relationship between fertility and household income is nonlinear. If this is so, the response of fertility to changes in household income is a function of the income level of the recipient. Further, if this response becomes more positive or less negative as income rises, then equalization of income levels among households results in lower aggregate fertility for the entire population. As a simple test of this, a quadratic relationship between fertility and household income per member can be specified, with the expectation of a negative linear term and a positive quadratic term.

Both in the direct and the reduced-form fertility equations, there is striking confirmation of this nonlinearity. For example, redistribution of income between households at one-half the average income level and households at five times the average level would reduce the overall fertility level by about 12 percent, approximately half a birth in terms of mean numbers of children ever born per household. It is clear from the income entries in table 4-26 that the nonlinear income effects operate both directly and through fertility-related norms.

The importance of the relatively egalitarian social structure on changes in Korean fertility is also shown through the associations of education and fertility. These are fully represented in the effects of parental educational status on the intermediate variables. Given these, there is no further impact of education on fertility. As the reduced-form coefficients indicate, for both parents, the greater difference occurs between the unschooled and those with basic education, followed by that between primary and middle-school graduates. This supports the suggestion that the government's provision of heavily subsidized, compulsory and universal primary education had a large impact on Korean fertility.

Several other findings of the earlier survey are reflected in the statistical results. For instance, it was suggested that for the individual household, a preference for sons has had a significant impact on fertility behavior. The estimated fertility equation supports this. Families with a higher proportion of living sons among their living children have tended to have fewer children than those who have a higher proportion of daughters. This indicates that the willingness to stop childbearing when desires for sons are fulfilled, as expressed in stated intentions and contraceptive practice, finds expression also in achieved fertility. While the effect of this preference for sons is not large (at the sample mean, the difference between all sons and all daughters would be .135 children per woman, or 4 percent of actual fertility), it is sufficiently systematic to be reliably estimated.

Also evident in the econometric analysis is an association between the household's child mortality experience and its fertility. Other things being equal, higher mortality is associated with higher fertility, when the former is expressed in terms, not of the number, but of the fraction of liveborn infants who have subsequently died. While the specification of this relation in the fertility equation is too crude to offer any insight to that already contributed by other research into this complex relationship, the findings do confirm the previous suggestion that the fall in child mortality over the period under study contributed to the fertility decline. The size of that relationship, however, as measured by the standardized regression coefficient, is evidently rather low although its reliability is high.

The historical study concluded that the shift of population from rural to urban places contributed to the decline in fertility. This finding has been confirmed. Rural residence, as reflected either in the place of origin or in the current farm occupation, is associated with higher fertility. Length of residence in one place, inversely related to migrant status, is also positively associated with fertility. It is interesting that residence and migration effects on fertility operate through many channels, including the formation of family-size norms and aspirations for children.

Another hypothesis from the historical study, which is supported by more formal analysis, is that the effects of female employment on fertility seem to operate mainly through the impact on age at marriage rather than on marital fertility. This is consistent with the more detailed data reported above.

In general, within the limits of this kind of cross-sectional household survey analysis, the results lend strong support to the earlier discussion. The analysis contributes additional insight into the mechanisms through which socioeconomic factors, and income changes especially, influence fertility. It underscores the point that income changes affect fertility in the long run through their effects on the demand for other goods and services and through the reallocation of household resources. Once these indirect effects are taken into consideration, as in the reduced-form equation, income effects on fertility appear stronger. In particular, the results illustrate the point that income growth at low-income levels raises household demand for education and the like. It follows, therefore, that interventions need not operate only by increasing the supply of schools and other services. Interventions that add to the incomes of low-income households will raise the demand for education and other services, and thus will also be effective. The impact of income, educational, and occupational variables supports the thesis that greater socioeconomic equality results in lower population fertility rates.

REFERENCES

Abraham, William I. 1976. "Observations on Korea's Income Distribution and the Adequacy of the Statistical Base" (Cambridge, Mass., Harvard Institute for International Development).

Ban, Sung Hwan, Pal Yong Moon, Dwight H. Perkins, Vincent Brandt,

Albert Keitel, and John Sloboda. 1979. *Studies in the Modernization of the Republic of Korea, 1945–1975: Rural Development,* Harvard East Asian Monograph no. 89 (Cambridge, Mass., Council on East Asian Studies, Harvard University).

Bendix, Reinhard, and Seymour Martin Lipset. 1966. *Class Status and Power* (New York, Free Press).

Brown, Gilbert T. 1973. *Korean Pricing Policies and Economic Development in the 1960s* (Baltimore, Md., The Johns Hopkins University Press).

Cho, Hyoung. 1976. "Women's Labor Force Participation in Korea." Paper presented at the East-West Center Summer Seminar on Population, Honolulu (July).

Cho, Jae Houp. 1964. "Post-1945 Land Reforms and Their Consequences in South Korea" (Ph.D. thesis, Indiana University, Bloomington).

Cole, David C., and Princeton N. Lyman. 1971. *Korean Development: The Interplay of Politics and Economics* (Princeton, N.J., Princeton University Press).

————, and Y. C. Park. 1975. "The Role of Financial Institutions in Korea's Economic Development, 1945–1975" (Cambridge, Mass., Harvard Institute for International Development).

Davis, Kingsley, and Judith Blake. 1956. "Social Structure and Fertility: An Analytic Framework" *Economic Development and Cultural Change,* vol. 4, pp. 211–235.

Donaldson, Peter. 1978. "The Evolution of the Korean Family Planning Program," in Robert Repetto, Kim Dae Young, Kuon Tae Hwan, Peter Donaldson, and Son Ung Kim, *Economic Development, Population Policy and the Demographic Transition in the Republic of Korea* (Cambridge, Mass., Harvard Institute for International Development).

Douglas, William A. 1962. "The Current Status of Korean Society" *Korean Affairs,* vol. 1, no. 4 (Seoul, Council on Korean Affairs).

Freedman, R., and L. C. Coombs. 1974. *Cross Cultural Comparisons on Two Factors in Fertility Behavior* (New York, The Population Council).

————, Tze-Huo San, Sou-Pen Wei, and Marybeth Weinberger. 1977. "Trends in Fertility and in the Effects of Education on Fertility in Taiwan 1961–74," *Studies in Family Planning* vol. 8, no. 1 (January) pp. 11–18.

Hasan, Parvez. 1976. *Korea, Problems and Issues in a Rapidly Developing Economy* (Baltimore, Md., The Johns Hopkins University Press for IBRD).

Hong, Sung-Bong. 1974. "Changing Patterns of Induced Abortion in South Korea," in *Population and Family Planning in the Republic of Korea,* vol. II (Seoul, Korean Institute for Family Planning).

International Bank for Reconstruction and Development (IBRD). 1976. "Population Growth and Human Resources Utilization in Korea" (Washington, D.C., IBRD).

————. 1977. *Prospects for Developing Countries, 1978–1985* (Washington, D.C., Development Policy Staff, IBRD).

Jain, Shail. 1975. *Size Distribution of Income: A Compilation of Data* (Washington, D.C., World Bank).

Korean Institute for Family Planning. 1974. *National Fertility Survey* (Seoul, KIFP).

————. 1973. *Report on 1971 Fertility-Abortion Survey* (Seoul, KIFP).

Kim, Nam-Il. 1977. "A Study of Cohort Fertility in Korea." Paper presented at the East–West Center Summer Seminar on Population, Honolulu (July).

Kim, Mo-Im, R. V. Rider, P. A. Harper, and J. M. Yang. 1974. "Changing Age at Marriage and the Influence of Social Demographic and Attitudinal Variables," *Population and Family Planning in the Republic of Korea,* vol. II (Seoul, Korean Institute for Family Planning).

Kim, Soo Kon. 1976. *Labor Force Behavior and Unemployment in Korea* (Seoul, Korean Development Institute).

Kim, Young Bong. 1977. "Education and Economic Growth," in Noel F. McGinn, Donald R. Snodgrass, Yong Bong Kim, Shin Bok Kim, Quee Yong Kim, *Studies in the Modernization of Korea, 1945–1975: Educational Development in Korea,* Harvard East Asian Monograph no. 90 (Cambridge, Mass., Council on East Asian Studies, Harvard University).

Kirk, Dudley. 1971. "A New Demographic Transition," *Rapid Population Growth,* prepared by the National Academy of Sciences (Baltimore, Md., The Johns Hopkins University Press).

Knodel, John. 1974. *The Decline of Fertility in Germany, 1871–1939* (Princeton, N.J., Princeton University Press).

Kwon, Tai Hwan. 1978. "The Historical Background to Korea's Demographic Transition," in Robert Repetto, Kwon Tai Hwan, Kim Son Ung, Peter Donaldson, and Kim Dae Young, *Economic Development, Population Policy, and the Demographic Transition in the Republic of Korea* (Cambridge, Mass., Harvard Institute of International Development).

Lee, Hae Young, Chang Yunskik, and Eui-Young Yu. 1975. *The Population of Korea* (Seoul, Seoul National University).

Lee, Hyo-Chai, and Cho Hyong. 1976. "Fertility and Women's Labor Force Participation in Korea," in *Recent Empirical Findings on Fertility: Korea, Nigeria, Tunisia, Venezuela, Philippines,* Occasional Monograph no. 7 (Washington, D.C., International Communications Program).

Lee, Hoon Koo, and Sung Jin Lee. 1973. "A Comparison of Early and Late Adoption of Family Planning," in *Psychological Studies in Population and Family Planning* (Seoul, Korean Institute for Research in Behavioral Sciences).

Lee, Man-Gap. 1976. "Socio-Cultural Context of Modernization in Korea" (Seoul, Seoul National University) Mimeo.

Mauldin, Parker, and Bernard Berelson. 1976. "Cross Cultural Review of the Effectiveness of Family Planning Programs" (Liege, Belgium, International Union for the Scientific Study of Population).

Mills, Edwin S., and Byung-Nah Song. 1979. *Studies in The Modernization of the Republic of Korea: 1945–1975: Urbanization and Urban Problems,* Harvard East-Asian Monograph no. 88 (Cambridge, Mass., Council on East Asian Studies, Harvard University).

Moon, Hyun-Sang, Seung-Hyun Han, and Soon Choi. 1973. *Fertility and Family Planning—An Interim Report on the 1971 Fertility–Abortion Survey* (Seoul, Korean Institute for Family Planning).

Pak, Ki Hyak, and others. 1966. *A Study of Land Tenure System in Korea* (Seoul, Korea Land Economics Research System).

Park, Chong Kee. 1976. *Social Security in Korea* (Seoul, Korean Development Institute).

Park, Hyoung Cho. 1973. *The Urban Middle Class Family in Korea* (Ph.D dissertation, Harvard University).

Park, J. H., and I. H. Park. 1976. "Migration and Female Labor Force Impact on Korean Fertility," in *The Dynamics of Migration* (Washington, D.C., Smithsonian Institution, International Communications Program).

Republic of Korea, Economic Planning Board. 1962. *Korea Statistical Yearbook* pp. 22–23. Also, 1960, 1966, and 1970.

Republic of Korea, Ministry of Agriculture. 1968 and 1974. *Yearbook of Agriculture and Forestry* (Seoul, Ministry of Agriculture).

Retherford, Robert D., and Nashiro Ogawa. 1976. "Decomposition of the Change in the Total Fertility Rate in the Republic of Korea, 1966–1970." Paper presented at the East–West Center 7th Summer Seminar on Population, Honolulu (June).

Ro, Kong-Kyun. 1976. "Migration and Fertility in Korea," in *The Dynamics of Migration* (Washington, D.C., Smithsonian Institution, International Communications Program).

Ross, John. 1976. "Transition in the Small Family, A Comparison of 1964–1973 Time Trends in Korea and Taiwan" (New York, Columbia University, Center for Population and Family Health).

Song, Kun Yom. 1973. "Birth Averted by Family Planning in Korea, 1960–70" (Seoul, Korean Institute for Family Planning).

Song, Kun Yong, and Seung Hyan Han. 1974. *National Family Planning and Fertility Survey: A Comprehensive Report* (Seoul, Korean Institute for Family Planning).

U.S. Bureau of the Census. 1978. *Country Demographic Profiles: Republic of Korea* (Washington, D.C., U.S. Bureau of the Census).

Watson, Walter, and Sung-Bong Hong. 1976. *The Increasing Utilization of Induced Abortion in Korea* (Seoul, Korea University Press).

Yoon, Jong-Joo. 1975. *A Study of the Population of Seoul* (Seoul, Ehwa Women's College).

Yu, Eui-Yong. 1973. "Components of Population Growth in Urban Areas of Korea: 1960–1970," *Bulletin of the Population and Development Studies Center* vol. II, nos. 1–2 (April).

5 ⏻ INTERNAL POLICIES FOR INCOME REDISTRIBUTION IN RURAL INDIA

INCOME DISTRIBUTION LEVEL AND TRENDS

Recent examinations of the association between economic growth and the distribution of income confirms the early generalization that disparities tend to widen in the early stages of development (Kuznets, 1963). These studies (Adelman and Morris, 1967; and Ahluwalia, 1976), however, also bring out another aspect of the association between inequalities and growth—the fact that the association is weak. At all levels of average income per capita, there are countries with relatively equal and unequal income distributions. According to Ahluwalia (1976, page 130), "Reorganizing the diversity of experience is perhaps the most important lesson to be drawn from the data." This diversity suggests that there are no general laws which determine the evolution of distributive shares, but rather that the pattern of development and the development policies or strategies adopted by the government shape the distribution of income which emerges.

This chapter explores factors underlying the distribution of income and internal policies for income distribution with reference primarily to rural India. Underlying this choice was (1) the need to give the discussion a definite focus and setting; (2) the salience of population concerns in India; (3) the importance of the Indian experience; and (4) the availability of informed and sophisticated analysis of the Indian experience by Indian social scientists.

This study draws heavily, but by no means exhaustively, on the impressive body of theoretical and empirical research which has been carried out by Indian scholars and others. In view of the complexity and scope of the Indian experience, the most that can be hoped from this chapter is that it may make a modest contribution to our greater understanding of certain aspects of the subject.

Efforts to understand the overall pattern of inequality and its changes over the postindependence period for all India have led to contradiction, because of differences in methodology and evidence (Kumar, 1974; Cassen, 1975; and Bardhan, 1974). Recent surveys emphasize that, while the available data tend to show narrowing disparities in income and in consumption expenditures during the 1950s and 1960s, these conclusions are tenuous. There are problems of differential price movements for different income classes, and underestimated income of indeterminate destination in the main data sources (Bardhan, 1974; Dandekar and Rath, 1971; Minhas, 1970; and Vaidyanathan, 1974).

Indirect evidence suggests a more pessimistic conclusion. In line with the surplus-labor model, asset prices—particularly of land—seem to have been raised by the growth process faster than real wages, which have, by and large, remained stable (Chaudri, 1974). The distribution of assets, especially in rural areas, has become more concentrated since 1960 (Pathak, Ganapathy, and Sarma, 1977; and Dasgupta, 1977). Rural-urban disparities seem to have risen, at least through the mid-sixties, while within the urban sector, the income share of property tended to rise (Ranadive, 1974). In the rural sector, although agricultural growth was labor-absorbing on balance (Raj Krishna, 1975; and Hanumantha Rao, 1975), employment does not seem to have risen faster than the growth of population (Cassen, 1975; and Chaudri, 1974). Because of the restricted range of the Green Revolution, interregional inequalities in the rural sector rose throughout the 1960s (Sanpath, 1975). According to Abel (1975), "While there appeared to be a trend toward reduction in inequalities in rural incomes during the 1950's, analysis for the 1960's would suggest that at best the distribution remained the same. However, some evidence suggests that inequalities actually increased."

This ambiguity suggests that particular areas should be examined in greater detail. Within areas affected by the high-yielding varieties technology, inequalities definitely seem to have increased (Rajaram, 1975; and Frankel, 1971). A number of village studies and resurveys indicate this (Cassen, 1975). Much of the analysis which follows is based on a resurvey of Matar Taluka in Gujerat State. The original survey was undertaken by J. C. Kumarappa in 1930, to explore the condition of the peasantry under the impact of the government's land-revenue policies. It resulted in a remarkably detailed portrait of living conditions, production, and landholdings in the area. Thirty-five years later it was decided to resurvey the area. Shri Vimal Shah was the director of the resurvey project. Out of this effort came a monograph by Shah and Shah of Bombay University, which provided a comprehensive picture of the changes which had taken place during the course of development.

The evidence of the resurvey indicated that although the general level of material well-being had risen in this part of Kaira District between 1929–30 and 1965–66, inequalities had substantially widened. The main findings were as follows:

Improvement of the standard of living of an average family in the Taluka was accompanied by unequal changes in the standard of living of families in different occupation groups. To begin with, there was wide inequality between different groups, and over thirty-five years it widened further. What was worse, while some groups prospered demonstrably, a few others experienced a decline in per capita expenditure. . . . Those who suffered a decline were small farmers with holdings below five acres, agricultural laborers, artisans, salary earners, and those in miscellaneous occupations. The rest consisted mostly of traders and cultivators of larger holdings who experienced an increase in per capita expenditures. Thus those who were producers or entrepreneurs and had control over some production assets or business could improve their standard of living. Others who provided mainly labor suffered in their standard of living. (Shah and Shah, 1974, pages 16–17)

Table 5-1 presents quantitative information in the extent of these changes. These figures should be regarded as merely indicative of trends, because of the uncertainty about the precise coverage of the earlier survey. Since it is likely that any sampling biases in the earlier work overrepresented middle- and upper-income households, the evidence on increasing inequalities may be an understatement of actual changes.

According to the estimates of the distribution of income in the two periods, the share of the poorest 20 percent of households fell from 4.1 percent to 2.6 percent of total household income between 1930–65. The share of the poorest 40 percent fell from 12.6 percent to 8.6 percent. At the same time, the share of the richest 20 percent households rose to 65 percent from 52.6 percent. This represents a substantial and adverse shift in the distribution of income over time.

In general, those who controlled only their own labor lost ground, while those who controlled capital and the means of production gained.

This phenomenon is more easily understood when it is realized that over this period, the population of Matar Taluka approximately doubled,

Table 5-1. Frequency Distribution of Household Income Per Annum for Selected Years

Fractile group (deciles)	1929–30		1965–66	
	Actual share	Cumulative share	Actual share	Cumulative share
Lowest	1.34	1.34	1.09	1.09
Second	2.76	4.10	1.49	2.58
Third	3.74	7.84	2.59	5.17
Fourth	4.78	12.62	3.39	8.56
Fifth	5.96	18.58	4.33	12.89
Sixth	7.50	26.08	5.57	18.46
Seventh	9.13	35.21	6.86	25.32
Eighth	12.20	47.41	9.47	34.79
Ninth	16.40	63.81	16.20	50.99
Highest	36.20	100.00	49.01	100.00

Source: Anil Deolalikar, "Poverty and Income Distribution in an Indian Taluka" (Cambridge, Mass., Harvard Center for Population Studies, November, 1975).

and has continued to increase at an accelerating pace. The burden of dependency, measured by the ratio of nonworkers to workers, rose substantially. At the same time, the amount of cultivable land available per capita fell from 1.65 to 0.95 acres (Shah and Shah, 1974, page 67). This was not accompanied by any perceptible fall in the average size of holdings, although the concentration of holdings substantially increased. Consequently, as the resurvey points out, "The bulk of the increase in the number of persons that belong to the erstwhile families of landholders would have been deprived of their land, and might have become landless. This is supported by the fact that the proportion of agricultural laborers which was 14.8 percent in 1911 and 17.7 percent in 1921 jumped to 26 percent in 1961" (Shah and Shah, 1974, page 11). In a manner paralleling occurrences in other areas of India, smallholders seem to have succumbed gradually to increasing burdens of debt and the fragmentation of their lands (Epstein, 1973; and Makherjee, 1971) which were absorbed by middle-sized and larger landowners. Matar Taluka became an area of increasing labor surplus, and real wages either stagnated or declined. In a manner which would have been readily comprehended by Malthus, Ricardo, or Marx, those with control over the increasingly scarce resources of the area prospered, while those competing on an ever more crowded labor market did not.

Table 5-2 presents information on the extent of the underlying shifts in the concentration of landholdings for the years 1929–30 and 1965–66.

Table 5-2. Frequency Distribution of Ownership of Land for Selected Years (in acres)

Fractile group (deciles)	1929–30		1965–66	
	Actual share	Cumulative share	Actual share	Cumulative share
Bottom	0.13	0.13	0.00	0.00
Second	1.27	1.40	0.00	0.00
Third	3.38	4.78	0.00	0.00
Fourth	4.68	9.46	0.20	0.20
Fifth	4.84	14.30	4.36	4.56
Sixth	9.69	23.99	5.29	9.85
Seventh	9.60	33.59	8.10	17.95
Eighth	13.88	47.47	13.35	31.10
Ninth	19.12	66.59	20.89	52.19
Tenth	33.41	100.00	48.00	100.00

Source: Anil Deolalikar, "Poverty and Income Distribution in an Indian Taluka" (Cambridge, Mass., Harvard Center for Population Studies, November, 1975).

The growing extent of landlessness is evident in table 5-2 from the fact that those in the bottom three deciles of farm households in 1965 owned no land at all. Thus, in 1965, at the start of the period of the Green Revolution, conditions had been created which promised further increases in inequalities as the result of rapid technological change. The larger landholders were in a position to gain from the rapid rise in land values and the opportunities for on-farm investment which followed the increase in potential farm yields and income. According to one knowledgeable observer, "The major cause of inequality in the distribution of income in rural areas is inequality in the ownership of land. This is true not only because land is the most important means of production but also because ownership of land is highly correlated with ease of access to institutions and the resources they provide" (Griffin, 1974a, page 188; and see also Ladejinsky, 1973, page A137; Bhalla, 1974; and Alamgir, 1975). The following section establishes quantitative estimates of the role of land distribution and other factors in income inequality in Matar Taluka.

SOURCES OF INCOME INEQUALITY

For the country as a whole, the disparity between the rural and urban sectors is a major source of inequality. Most of the poor are rural residents, in India as elsewhere (Chenery and coauthors, 1974, chapter V; Dandekar and Rath, 1971; and Schuh, 1975). Much of this disparity is attributable to a pervasive policy bias against the rural sector, expressed through numerous policy instruments (Bhagwati and Srinavasan, 1974; and International Labour Organisation, 1974). Within the rural sector, regional disparities are important. They widened in India during the 1960s, essentially because the benefits of high-yielding varieties of food grains, which encouraged intensification of farming techniques, have been restricted to areas of assured water supplies; mostly, to acreage under irrigation.

These developments are discernible even at the local level. Shah and Shah (1974), in their resurvey of Matar Taluka, found that interregional differentials in per capita income, which had been minimal in 1929–30, had widened substantially by 1965–66. The region within the taluka with the largest area under irrigation experienced much faster growth in agricultural and total output per capita. The consequence was a widening of interregional disparities. This affected mostly landholding families. The productivity of land and capital increased much faster in irrigated than in dry regions. Because of the overall labor surplus in the region and the constancy of real wage rates, there was little increase in inequalities among agricultural laborers' households between regions over the periods 1929–30 and 1965–66. With agricultural labor in elastic supply, technological change has raised the returns to land, water, and capital, the inelastic inputs, much more than it has affected real wage rates. Consequently, within the rural sector, inequalities among households are substantially determined by the concentration of assets, principally land and other capital.

This economic structure necessitates a framework for the analysis of income formation which differs from that usually employed in the industrial countries. There, where earned income is the main source for most people, attention is focused on differences in the stock of human capital resources. Those account for differences in wage and salary levels among workers. Years of formal schooling and on-the-job training account for a large percentage of the variation in earnings among full-time workers. In rural India, however, there is considerable underemployment, a great deal of work is relatively undifferentiated labor in which years of experience account for little additional productivity beyond some point, and income includes a substantial return on owned assets. Fortunately, the data available for Matar Taluka includes substantial information on the households' tangible assets—land, buildings, equipment, and stock.

The hypothesis that the income per capita of each household was a return on household resources, consisting of physical capital, human capital, and labor resources, was tested. Physical capital was measured by (1) the value of land per capita, and (2) the value of other tangible assets less the amount of household debt outstanding. It was realized that the use of a value measure to represent landholdings involves the problem that land is itself valued on local capital markets in terms of its future income potential, so that in the aggregate causality flows the other way from income to asset value. However, the use of a physical measure would have required the creation of such a detailed index, measuring various quality dimensions, for which data were not available in the survey, that this alternative was ruled out as infeasible.

The human capital resources available to the household were measured in terms of the years of formal schooling of adult household members. Two levels of education, primary and secondary, were distinguished and measured, respectively, by the proportion of adult household male members educated up to the fifth through the seventh standard, and the proportion of adult males (fourteen years of age or older) who had matriculated. These variables embody the underlying concept of the household as an income-pooling community, such that the relevant measure of household resources is the proportion of economically active members with given educational attainments. It was decided, as a recognition of fact, to focus on male adults, because few women are economically active outside the domestic sphere. Even so, the use of years of exposure to formal schooling as a measure of the acquisition of economically useful skills is probably inadequate in the context of rural India. It should be remembered, however, that both age and caste, which still has strong occupational implications, also reflect the distribution of nonformal occupational training. Table 5-3 gives the distribution of educational attainment in Matar Taluka.

Caste was included as a measure of the fragmentation of labor markets, on the hypothesis that discrimination would lead to a higher income for higher-caste households, irrespective of their other characteristics. The castes represented in the resurvey were grouped into only two classifications: high caste, consisting of Patidars, Garasias, Brahmins, and others; and low caste, consisting of Dharalas, Muslims, Shepherds, and Harijans. As an alternative approach to the investigation of this hypothesis, the sample was also partitioned on the basis of caste, and the

Table 5-3. Distribution of Primary and Secondary Education

No. of adult males in household with primary education	Total number of adult males	Percentage of total males	Cumulative frequency (%)
Zero	1,235	72.0	72.0
1	374	21.9	93.9
2	93	5.4	99.3
3	9	0.5	99.8
4	4	0.2	100.0

Distribution of Secondary Education

No. of adult males in household with secondary education	Total number of adult males	Percentage of total males	Cumulative frequency (%)
Zero	1,587	92.6	92.6
1	105	6.1	98.7
2	21	1.2	99.9
3	1	0.1	100.0

Source: Calculated from unpublished data from Resurvey of Matar Taluka.

relation of household income per capita to the other variables was explored for each caste group separately.

The age of the head of the household was also included as a determinant of income, in order to reflect the life-cycle effect so often observed elsewhere, and to act as a crude indicator of the acquisition of relevant skills with experience. In order to adequately represent the life-cycle of earnings, it was necessary to include a quadratic term in the age of the head of the household.

Similarly, to test the hypothesis that there are diminishing returns to landholding size, or higher returns per acre on smaller farms, as so often is reported in farm surveys, a nonlinear term in land value per capita was introduced. Other nonlinearities were admitted to encompass possible interaction effects between human and physical capital holdings of the household, and other interactions, such as that of caste with assets or land with other tangible assets. In general, it was postulated that all forms of household resources should be complementary, so that position interaction effects were expected.

Following the literature on human capital, the natural logarithm of household income per capita was regressed on the set of explanatory variables described above. Because of the fact that 1965–66 (the year of the

Table 5-4. Regression of the Logarithm of Total Family Income Per Capita on Household Resources

Explanatory variable	Regression coefficient	F statistic	Beta coefficient
Land value per capita	.00045	364.4	.81
Land value per capita squared	−.00001	61.5	−.36
Other net assets per capita	.00014	104.8	.34
Fraction of adult males with primary schooling	.11	5.7	.04
Fraction of adult males with secondary schooling	.83	11.3	.16
Age of head	.011	3.0	.16
Age of head, squared	−.00015	4.8	−.21
Nonworking children per capita	−.48	42.2	−.12
Caste	.12	10.6	.06

Note: $R^2 = .49$; degrees of freedom, 1,690.

resurvey) was a disastrous agricultural year for most of India, it was decided that the reported household income of that year, which included income both in kind and in cash from market and nonmarket production, might include a large disturbance element. Therefore, the level of total consumption expenditure per capita, also including the value of home-produced goods and services (to some extent), was also used as an indicator of permanent household income, since, as is well known, consumption is more stable in the face of short-term fluctuations than is income.

The results of the regression analysis, given in tables 5-4 and 5-5, do much to reinforce one's confidence in both the model and the data on which it is estimated. With income per capita used as the dependent variable, the model accounts for one-half of the actual cross-sectional variance. All explanatory variables are of the expected sign and significantly differ from zero, with the exception of the interaction terms representing the interaction of caste and education, land and education, and land and other assets, which are either insignificantly different from zero or, in the case of the last, very small.

As expected, differences in landholding per capita account for a major part of income differentials in the sample, which includes agricultural households. There is evidence of diminishing returns to larger farm holdings. The distribution of other tangible assets also plays a major role in the formation of household income, as would be expected.

Table 5-5. Regression of the Logarithm of Total Household Consumption
Expenditures Per Capita on Household Resources

Explanatory variable	Regression coefficient	F statistic	Beta coefficient
Land value per capita	.00021	173	.59
Land value per capita squared	− .00001	18	− .21
Other net assets per capita	.00008	76	.31
Fraction of adult males with primary schooling	.13	17	.08
Fraction of adult males with secondary schooling	.50	8.7	.15
Age of head	.011	6.5	.25
Age of head, squared	− .00012	7.2	− .26
Nonworking children per capita	− .49	93	− .18
Caste	.12	23	.09

Note: $R^2 = .44$; degrees of freedom, 1,690.

Also, as hypothesized, the educational resources commanded by the household are positively related to income per capita, and the return to secondary education is perceptibly higher than the return to primary education.

The life-cycle effect of age is evident: income tends to rise and then level off, or decline as the age of the head of the household increases. The effects of the dependency burden are equally evident. Households in which a larger fraction of household members are nonworking children tend to have lower household income per capita, as one might expect. At least, this finding eliminates the possibility that the incentive effect effectively spurs the adult earners to extra efforts in order to maintain or increase the level of per capita income in the presence of dependent children.

Finally, the effects of caste are as expected. Other things being equal, higher-caste households with equal resources have higher incomes than lower-caste households. This can be interpreted as the persistence of fragmentation or discrimination in the relevant markets, or the positive association of caste with other omitted variables, such as aspirations, unmeasured resources, and the like.

This model permits the decomposition of the inequality of income in terms of the inequality in the distribution of determining elements. The determining elements in the model are the explanatory variables discussed above, all of which are, in relation to current income per capita, either exogenous or predetermined. From the regression equation, taking variances on both sides, one can express the variance of the logarithm of

Table 5-6. Decomposition of Log Household Income Per Capita in Terms of
Variances and Covariances

Explanatory factors	Variance associated with explanatory factors							
	(1)	(2)	(3)	(4)	(5)	(6)	(7)	(8)
(1) Other net assets	.109							
(2) Land value	.280	.609						
(3) Age of head	.023	.052	.025					
(4) Age squared	−.031	−.069	−.063	.042				
(5) Caste	.009	.010	.002	−.003	.004			
(6) Dependent children	.010	.016	.008	−.011	.000	.013		
(7) Education: matriculation	.018	.022	.000	−.001	+.004	.000	.024	
(8) Education: primary	.004	.007	.001	−.001	.001	−.001	.001	.002

Note: Predicted variance, 1.116; predicted variance associated with the variances of factors, .828.

household income per capita in terms of the variances and covariances of the regressors. Symbolically,

$$\mathrm{Var}\left(\log\frac{Y}{P}\right) = \sum_{i=1}^{k}\sum_{j=1}^{k} \hat{b}_i\hat{b}_j \, \mathrm{Cov}\,(X_iX_j) \tag{5-1}$$

where the $\hat{b}_i$ are the estimated regression coefficients, and the covariance of an explanatory variable X_i with itself is its variance. In these terms, the effect of any of the income-determining variables on the inequality of incomes can be expressed as the consequence of three influences: the strength of its influence on the level of income; its variance over the population; and the strength of its covariances with other important income-determining variables.

Analysis of the inequality of incomes in Matar Taluka within this framework yields interesting insights into some of the underlying forces. Table 5-6 presents the decomposition of the distribution of permanent household income per capita. The predicted variance on the basis of the estimated regression equation is 1.1. Of the total predicted inequality, table 5-6 shows that most is associated with the variances of the explanatory variables themselves, indicated by the elements along the diagonal. The sum of variances is 0.83, which is 77 percent of the predicted inequality. The reason for this is simple to understand: the correlations among the explanatory variables over the sample are not particularly high, with few exceptions. Therefore, the effects of variances predominate.

Of the contributing factors, it is easily recognized that the inequality in the distribution of landholdings by far dominates as a source of income inequality in Matar Taluka. Its direct effect, 0.61, accounts for 60 percent of predicted inequality. Moreover, it shows strong covariance effects with the other factors, particularly net assets other than land, which is by itself the second most important source of inequality, accounting for 10 percent of predicted inequality. Not only is this finding completely in accordance with other research findings, it is readily comprehensible in terms of the data presented in this analysis: landholdings play a major role in the determination of household income, and the variance in the distribution of land is relatively large.

By comparison, the influence of other factors is very small. The effect of the age distribution is negligible, because of the nonlinear life cycle of earnings. The small influence of caste is attributable largely to its relatively small effect on income, other things being equal. By contrast, the small effect of variations in the dependency burden is more largely attributable to the small variance in the proportion of nonworking children among households. The small effect of the education measures is caused in substantial part by both: in rural Gujerat, education plays a relatively minor part in determining income levels, and there is relatively little variance among households in educational standing.

As is evident in table 5-6, only the interaction between the distributions of land and other assets, which are positively correlated, contributes significantly to the total inequality of income per capita. This occurs because of the substantial importance of both these factors and their substantial correlation, 0.54, in the sample.

The results suggest that substantial changes in the distribution of income in rural areas like Matar Taluka would be difficult to achieve without a change in the distribution of land ownership. At present, there is not a great deal of variation among the sample households in the proportion of adult males educated up to primary or secondary levels. A rise in educational enrollment would probably entail, at least for a generation or more, an *increase* in the variation of educational attainment, since substantial cohort differentials would be introduced into the population.

Similarly, in the sample households there is relatively little variation in the proportion of nonworking children, so that a fall in fertility— unless it were distributed evenly across households—might initially increase the variance of this factor. Moreover, neither the demographic nor educational strategy seems to have sufficient impact on rural household income per capita. If these results are of the right order of magnitude, only a redistribution of assets is likely to make an appreciable impact on the distribution of rural incomes.

This analysis certainly confirms and reinforces the view that land reform is an important, perhaps essential, policy of income redistribution in rural areas of developing countries. It supports the statement of Griffin (1975, page 328), "The inevitable conclusion is that virtually the only way of significantly improving the distribution of income in rural areas within a relatively short period of five years is by redistributing the stock of wealth; i.e., essentially, land."

Nonetheless, there have been several serious and well-considered arguments made against a policy of land reform as an instrument of income redistribution, both for India and for less-developed countries in general. Given the scarcity of land and the vast numbers of landless peasants and very small farms, even a drastic redistribution would permit the establishment of a minimum holding so small that large numbers of households would be left below the poverty line, having holdings incapable of providing a minimum standard of living. Full implementation of the existing ceiling legislation in India, implying redistribution of holdings in excess of 20 acres to the smallest farmers, would leave 60 percent of these beneficiaries below the poverty line, while leaving untouched the situation of the rural households without any land at all (Minhas, 1970, page 401). Such a policy, it is argued, would hardly dent the dimensions of rural poverty, while creating a large number of new, uneconomical smallholdings which would either be inefficiently farmed or soon sold out to bigger farmers. The point has been even more forcefully made by Dandekar and Rath (1971, page 469), authors of a comprehensive study of poverty in India: "However, the dimensions of rural poverty are such that . . . distribution of the available land among all those who need it can do little good to the poor and can do undoubted harm to the prospects of agricultural development generated by recent technical advances."

Implementation of the sort of ceilings legislation that is now in force in India would have a substantial impact on income distribution. This has been confirmed by a simulation of such a land redistribution in Matar Taluka. Using the data from Shah and Shah (1974), it was supposed that surplus land from all holdings in excess of 25 acres would be redistributed to farm households without land or with holdings smaller than 3 acres.

This redistribution would be sufficient to provide all farm households with a minimum holding of 3 acres. It would have the effect of reducing the variance of landholding by 65 percent. The effects on the redistribution of incomes were estimated, assuming an equal reduction in the variance of landholdings in terms of value. (This might be something of an exaggeration, since there would be a tendency for large farmers to release their poorest land for redistribution.) Assuming that the land redistribution would be accompanied by sufficient provision for credit and ancillary services, that the correlation between land- and other assetholding would be undistributed, and by ignoring other covariances as quantitatively unimportant, the direct consequence of the specified land redistribution would be a reduction in the variance of the logarithm of household income by 0.4, out of a predicted baseline variance of 1.12. This amounts to a 34 percent reduction of predicted income inequality. Despite the oversimplification of its assumptions, this simulation indicates that a land redistribution would be capable of a substantial reduction in the degree of income inequality.

It is unnecessary to rely on simulation exercises, however, when the evidence of successful land redistribution is available. The experience of the Republic of Korea provided one example of this. A study of land reform in Egypt concluded that successive reforms between 1952–61 lowered the Gini coefficient of concentration of land ownership from .61 in 1951 to .38 in 1965. Correspondingly, and partly because of the medium-run impact of tenancy regulations, substantial redistribution of farm income was achieved: the share of small cultivators with less than five feddan in total farm income rose from 10 to 37 percent from 1950 to 1961, while the share of farmers with more than 50 feddan and that for absentee landlords fell to 19 percent from 30 percent (Abdel-Fahid, 1975, page 48). Another recent study of land reform, in the People's Republic of China, estimated that the redistribution of land and the cancellation of owner's debts, which affected 44 percent of the arable land in China, directly redistributed 17 percent of gross domestic product, or about 26 percent of value added in agriculture. This income came from the rents and returns to management and, to a small extent, labor of the large farmer and absentee owner. It went in about equal shares to the peasant who received the redistribution land, and to the state (Lippitt, 1974, pages 79 and 122).

The redistributive impact of this successful land reform can be judged by the fact that, throughout the world, the average share in total

Table 5-7. Resource Utilization on Large and Small Holdings in Matar Taluka, 1965–66

Size class (acres per household member)	Working females as % of total females in household	Working children as % of total children in household	Casual labor income as % of total income	Casual labor income as % of total income
0.00–0.59	52	5.5	24	13
0.60–1.00	30	5.9	10	13
1.00–3.00	21	2.6	2	8
3.00–5.00	5	0.0	0	4
Over 5	17	0.0	0	4

Source: Calculated from unpublished data of Vimal Shah and C. H. Shah.

household income of the poorest 40 percent of households is approximately 15 percent, and in countries with very unequal distributions of income it may be as low as 6 to 8 percent. In other words, the income redistributed through reform in China probably doubled the average income of the recipients. To dismiss such a change as an insubstantial contribution to the reduction of rural poverty is to miss the point made by Sen (1974) that it is not just the *number* of households below some poverty line which is of concern but also the *extent* to which the households fall below it. A policy which doubles the incomes of households in the lowest-income strata is a powerful instrument, whether or not those households afterwards emerge above some arbitrarily established poverty line.

Concepts like the poverty line or the minimum viable size of holding can be misused. There is no clear-cut borderline of viability, or of an uneconomic holding. Rather, there is a continuum ranging from extreme poverty to affluence. Households on the smallest holdings adapt to their situation of resource scarcity by utilizing more intensively all that they have. The smaller the amount of land available per capita, the greater the labor force-participation rates of women and children, who must engage in market labor to supplement household income; the greater the importance of casual wage earnings as a fraction of total household income; and the greater the importance of income from labor-intensive animal husbandry. At the margin, households with little land derive a high proportion of income from nonagricultural activities. Additional land made available to the household, by adding to its stock of productive resources, permits a higher level of income. The fact that redistribution of land can only make those at the bottom less poor, rather than well-to-do, is by no means an argument against redistribution.

It has also been argued that a redistribution of income and wealth through a land reform would adversely affect the overall rate of savings, thus indirectly lowering the rate of capital accumulation and growth. For example, there is evidence that savings rates are higher out of nonlabor incomes than out of labor incomes. Household surveys also indicate that savings are concentrated in the upper income groups.

This argument has been attacked from several directions. It can be demonstrated that poverty forces households to sell out the future in order to survive the present. The more inadequate landholdings are, the more debt households are forced to incur for consumption purposes relative to income, and the less households are able to invest in their children's future through education. Also, the more inadequate landholdings are, the less able households are to preserve their own future health by maintaining an adequate level of nutritional intake. In short, poverty forces households to disinvest. When resources are made available, households stop disinvesting in themselves. At the margin, the rate of savings and investment of low-income households is high, perhaps at least as high as that of high-income households.

Moreover, as demonstrated by the Chinese experience, the transfer of income confiscated from large landowners in a land reform is a matter of policy choice, in large part. Either through direct taxation of land or produce, or through manipulation of the terms of trade between farm output and other commodities, governments are able to extract a portion of the additional income which would otherwise flow to the beneficiaries of the land reform. In China, this apparently amounted to roughly one-half of the total income transfer, or as much as 8 percent of the gross domestic product. This represents a very substantial fraction of aggregate annual savings, and demonstrates that it would be possible to compensate through public savings should there be any tendency for total household savings to decline (Lippitt, 1974, page 122).

Another argument against a land redistribution is its potentially adverse effect on agricultural output. A large increase in the number of holdings and fraction of total acreage in the smallest-size class suggests to some that the efficiency of operations and the pace of technological advance would be restrained (Dandekar and Rath, 1971; and Warriner, 1969). They point out that larger farmers are the first to innovate and that they have the resources to utilize "lumpy" inputs and to spread out unavoidable risks.

However, the high-yielding varieties technology is essentially scale neutral. The difference in techniques employed on large and smallholdings is in large part a rational response to differences in the scarcities or prices of inputs that are faced by large and small farmers. Most small holders, largely because of insecure tenures and lack of influence in local institutions, must borrow to purchase fertilizers and pesticides at informal market rates of 2 or 3 percent per month. At the same time they have, at the margin, surplus labor during much of the year. By contrast, large holders are much more likely to obtain institutional credit on more favorable terms, but are likely to require hired labor. These substantial differences in relative input prices make it rational for small farmers to use more labor-intensive methods, and for large farmers to make more use of working capital and purchased inputs (Griffin, 1974a, page 189).

This can be illustrated with information from Matar Taluka. There, despite having relatively less access to irrigation, small farms obtain as high yields and produce as great a value of output per acre as do large farms. The total value of inputs, including relatively large amounts of unpaid family labor is greater on smaller farms.

In Matar Taluka, the situation with respect to credit distribution deteriorated between the date of the initial survey and the resurvey in 1966. Although during both periods the small farmer was more deeply in debt, as measured in terms of land or annual crop value, the larger farmer between the periods had increased his indebtedness to a greater extent and had devoted a larger percentage of his borrowings to productive purposes. Moreover, the large farmer had been able to obtain a far greater share of his credit needs from cooperative societies and the land development bank and was far less dependent on the local moneylenders than was the small farmer. This represents something of a perverse shift from the situation which existed in 1930, when the small farmer actually obtained a larger share of his credit needs from institutional sources, primarily cooperative societies and *taccavi* loans from the government (Shah and Shah, 1974, page 138).

The adverse impact of credit rationing against small farmers can be demonstrated. In the 1965–66 resurvey, careful information concerning current borrowings and indebtedness, the use of agricultural inputs, and land use, agricultural output, and productivity, was collected from the sample of 830 farm households. The specific hypothesis, that access to institutional credit, particularly for the small farmer, would be associated with a greater use of modern agricultural inputs, was tested. Since the availability of institutional credit is actually the constraint, if for no other reason than that the interest charges on institutional loans are far below those in the informal sector, it was reasonable to proceed on the assumption that differences among households in use of institutional credit reflected primarily supply, and not demand, variations. At the same time, access to credit is only one of several important factors which influence the use of modern inputs. The availability of an assured water supply through irrigation is another very important influence. Again, since in Matar Taluka almost all the irrigation water is obtained from canals, and since canal water is by far the cheapest water source if it is available, it was safe to assume that the variations among farmers in the use of irrigation reflected mainly supply, not demand, variation. Finally, the size of holding, for reasons already discussed, including risk, indivisibilities in input supply, and differentials in the capacity for self-finance, influences the use of purchased inputs. Consequently, in order to control for these other influences, the sample of cultivator households was partitioned by size of holding into small (less than 5 acres), medium-sized (5 to 15 acres), and large (more than 15 acres) landholders. In addition, each category was subdivided into irrigated and unirrigated holdings. Finally, each subcategory was further divided into holdings with use of institutional credit and holdings without the use of modern inputs. The use of modern inputs was measured by the percentage of the holding to which chemical fertilizer was applied, since, at this period, this was the most important nontraditional input in this area.

The results have been reported in Table 5-8. They are clear-cut. A greater percentage of large farmers had access to institutional credit. Across all other categories, cultivators with irrigated holdings used chemical fertilizers to a substantially greater extent than did cultivators without irrigation. Across all other categories, cultivators with larger holdings used chemical fertilizers to a greater extent than did those with smaller holdings.

This is entirely in accordance with expectations. Yet, it is instructive to look further into the detailed results. Table 5-8 also indicates that greater use of fertilizer is strongly associated with access to institutional credit, especially for small farmers. For them, fertilizer use is almost twice as prevalent for farmers with institutional borrowings. For medium-sized

Table 5-8. Access to Credit and Use of Chemical Fertilizers by Size of Farm, Irrigation, and Access to Institutional Credit

Type of holding	Number of holdings	Mean fraction of area under fertilizers	Standard deviation
Holdings under 5 acres	236	.16	.323
Without irrigation	135	.07	.257
Without institutional credit	106	.06	.247
With institutional credit	30	.12	.29
Percentage with institutional credit	22.2		
With irrigation	101	.28	.36
Without institutional credit	78	.25	.35
With institutional credit	22	.41	.39
Percentage with institutional credit	21.8		
Holdings from 5 to 15 acres	248	.25	.26
Without irrigation	69	.08	.16
Without institutional credit	46	.08	.16
With institutional credit	23	.08	.17
Percentage with institutional credit	33.3		
With irrigation	180	.31	.27
Without institutional credit	110	.31	.28
With institutional credit	69	.32	.24
Percentage with institutional credit	38.3		
Holdings larger than fifteen acres	112	.35	.27
Without irrigation	7	.13	.19
Without institutional credit	4	.05	.09
With institutional credit	3	.23	.25
Percentage with institutional credit	42.8		
With irrigation	105	.37	.26
Without institutional credit	57	.37	.27
With institutional credit	48	.37	.26
Percentage with institutional credit	45.7		

Source: Calculated from unpublished data of Vimal Shah and C. H. Shah.

and large farms with irrigation, the differences are insignificant. For large landholders, only for those without irrigation is there a strong association between institutional borrowing and fertilizer use, but there are few farms in this category. The results demonstrate that lack of access to institutional credit is an obstacle to small farmers in the adoption of modern practices, and that access to institutional credit was strongly associated with the size of landholding.

Further, small farmers with access to institutional credit and with irrigated holdings were the most likely to be using fertilizer in 1965, at the outset of the Green Revolution. This contradicts the assertion that small farmers are necessarily slow to innovate, but is consistent with the experience of other rural economies with equally distributed land (Griffin, 1974a).

An argument of quite another sort against a policy of land redistribution, one which runs directly against the grain of the evidence that more equal distributions promote lower fertility, is the contention that a redistribution of land would have a pronatalist effect resulting, at least in the short run, in a higher birth rate (Rosenzweig and Evenson, 1976; Simon, 1972; and Simon, 1974, pages 89–91). This conclusion is based on evidence from pre-World War II China, from India, from nineteenth-century Poland, from fifteenth-century Italy, and from the contemporary Philippines, indicating a positive association between the cumulative fertility of farm wives and the size of household farm holdings. There are also studies, such as one of fertility differentials in Turkey, which find fertility related to the size of landholdings in the familiar U-shaped pattern (Timur, 1971).

This static cross section contradicts both the aggregative and disaggregated evidence that more equal distributions of income are associated with lower fertility, and the historic evidence of the consequences of land reform in developing countries like Korea. In none of the countries in which thoroughgoing land reform has been carried through has there been a subsequent sustained increase in fertility. On the contrary, fertility has declined, usually at a more rapid pace. The redistribution of landed wealth, implying equalization of incomes as well as social and political relations, seems to have been at least a contributing factor to the subsequent rapid declines in fertility in the rural areas.

Part of the problem is that it is misleading to regard a household with a larger holding as being richer than one with a smaller holding, since in societies with extended kinship relations, a larger holding may have to support a greater number of relatives. The more relevant measure of wealth is the availability of resources per household number. It is the availability of per capita assets which in large part determines the level of per capita income, and it is per capita income which influences living standards and fertility.

When fertility is measured against the size of holdings, defined in terms of acreage available per household member, there is a strong inverse relationship between the size of the holding and fertility. This is apparent in the survey data from Matar Taluka (table 5-9).

Table 5-9.   The Relationship Between Current Fertility and the Size of Holding, Matar Taluka, 1965–66

(in Cultivated Acres per Household Member)

Size of holding	Fertility; children aged zero to 5, per women aged 15–45	Total family size
0.00–0.59	0.792	6.82
0.60–1.00	0.761	6.21
1.00–3.00	0.711	5.90
3.00–5.00	0.627	5.70
Over 5.00	0.329	3.90

Source: Calculated from unpublished data of Vimal Shah and C. H. Shah.

Table 5-10.   Fertility and Total Family Size by Absolute Size of Farm, in Matar Taluka, 1965–66

Size of holding (total acres)	Fertility: Children zero to 5 per women aged 15–45	Total family size
0–3	.625	5.1
3–5	.677	5.1
5–10	.732	5.9
10–15	.732	6.7
15–25	.744	7.1
Over 25	.774	8.9

Source: Vimal Shah and C. H. Shah, Resurvey of Matar Taluka (Bombay, Vora Publishers, 1974) p. 60; and unpublished resurvey data.

By contrast, when farm size is measured without reference to the number of persons it supports, there appears to be a positive association between fertility and family size, as shown in table 5-10. This illustrates how important it is to choose the proper measure of economic status.

Indirect evidence of another sort also suggests that a redistribution of property rights to land would be antinatalist. It has been shown that poverty forces households to disinvest, to sell out the future in favor of the present, and this also may apply to family size. If children are assets, they are inferior ones. Under conditions of rapid population growth and technological change, for example, investment in land is much more profitable than investment in additional labor. The expected return to the "investment" in additional children has been shown to be low, or even negative, in conditions of peasant agriculture (Mueller, 1976). When indebtedness to moneylenders at high rates of interest is common, large family size is more often associated with downward rather than upward mobility. According to Warriner (1969, page 149), "In the propertied class of a *ryotwari* village there is a continual upward and downward movement among the landholders owing to the Hindu law of succession which prescribes equal division of landed property among sons; the landholders with prolific families tend to sink deeper into poverty, while those producing few children tend to grow wealthy." Fragmentation of land, and the necessity to go into debt for dowries for the daughters, have undermined family fortunes for many Indian smallholders. Consequently, when households are given access to a superior asset, such as agricultural land, the motivation for a large family as a means of long-term security may diminish. This is consistent with the Korean experience: there is strong evidence that Korean households, when given the opportunity, have chosen investments in land and their children's education over large families. It is also consistent with the substitution effect between male children and other assets found in a study of long-term savings behavior in Matar Taluka (Shah and Repetto, 1975).

Another criticism leveled against a policy of redistribution through land reform is that, in most parts of the developing world, it cannot be adopted and carried through without a drastic prior realignment of political power. If the ruling party or class has a good part of its political support in the rural areas among the larger farmers, as in India, and these larger farmers, in turn, receive most of the benefits from government activities in the rural areas, it is impossible for the government to destroy its own political base without destroying itself. It cannot be expected that it will do so. The historical evidence fully supports this view. Land reforms, to the extent they have been carried out at all in the past, have tended to benefit primarily the medium-sized and larger farmers. According to Byres (1974, page 247), "The present configuration of political forces in India effectively precludes redistribution; it is a configuration which derives from the agrarian structure which land reform, as implemented, has helped create."

Historical evaluations of the implementation of land reform in India generally conclude that so far it has had only limited impact. Large absentee holdings have largely been eliminated, and a class of substantial proprietors has been stabilized in their tenurial rights (Warriner, 1969, page 166). However, widespread loopholes and tax implementation of tenancy reform in most areas have resulted in evictions, resumption of land by the owner, and the evasion of the intention of the legislation to return the "land to the tiller," so that small landholders and sharecroppers in most areas have benefited little (Byres, 1974, page 247; and Srinavasan, 1974, page 372). In an analysis of the implementation of tenancy legislation in sample areas of western India, including the region of Matar Taluka, it was found that tenancy reform had resulted in little or no change in the size distribution of holdings. However, there was a sizable increase in the percentage of farm operators who owned their holdings (Dantwala and Shah, 1971, pages 65–68), and of those who were landholders at the time of the survey, small landholders and previously landless peasants were, on balance, gainers of land while large landholders were the losers. These findings must be seen, however, against the backdrop of rising landlessness among agricultural households and the increasing concentration of landholdings over a longer period of time. Dantwala and Shah (1971, page 117) concluded their investigation with the realization that greater equality in the distribution of landholdings could not be brought about through the redistribution of land held under tenancy arrangements, but would require the redistribution of owner-cultivated property.

The history of legislation regarding ceilings on landholdings in India is, if anything, more discouraging. Loopholes were written into the laws in most states, and implementation of the law has been ineffective. As a consequence, only about 500,000 ha have ever been redistributed, with negligible impact on the distribution of holdings or on the extent of landlessness in rural India (Srinavasan, 1974, page 372). The experience of three five-year planning periods were recently summed up in the *Economic and Political Weekly* (1975, page 1494) as follows, "It is by now widely known and even the Government has recognized that land reforms have hardly helped to bring about any significant redistribution of land in favor of the poor."

In the face of this unsuccessful experience, the feasibility of tenurial reform as a redistributive strategy in India is certainly questionable. It has been acknowledged that an approach based on legislation from above will fail in the absence of effective organization and participation on the part of the peasantry, the lack of an effective political coalition against the landed interests, and the lack of a sociopolitical context which affords all classes a reasonable degree of access to legal resource. In concluding his penetrating review of land-reform studies in India, Joshi (1975, page 101) has said, "If there is one single lesson of land reform implementation in the past, it is that the consciousness and organization of the peasantry, and the support of strategic sectors of society . . . is crucial."

Joshi also points out, however, that pessimistic assessments typically ignore the dynamic elements and possibilities of change in agrarian relations. One of these has been the commercialization and capitalization of agricultural production itself. The Green Revolution has accelerated the transformation of agricultural production into a commercial undertaking based on purchased inputs and borrowed funds, relying heavily on wage labor for peak-season operations. The resumption of lands and the importance of the owner-cultivator in affected areas have also contributed to the weakening of patron-client bonds and traditional obligations in the rural sector. As a consequence, while disparities have increased, the functional basis and perceived legitimacy of inequalities have been eroded (Frankel, 1971; and Joshi, 1975). The results have included an increased class awareness and have accentuated polarization of rural society along the lines of the haves and have-nots. These changes are conducive to the organization and emergence of the rural poor as a political force.

In India, a second element has been the weakening of the traditional Congress party machine, which is based largely on rural interests in the state governments, as a political force in national politics. The national party leader's ability to establish an effective power base in the support of urban, industrial, military, and bureaucratic groups, by means of a direct populist appeal to the masses, created a power bloc independent of and opposed to landed interests. As a consequence, the central government increasingly favored agrarian reform and pressed for more effective action, including the initiation of a number of programs intended specifically to benefit and strengthen the marginal farmer. Such changes can mobilize the energies of affected groups as a force for further change. This has been, by and large, the experience of Kerala, where there has been the most popular participation in land reform of all the Indian states (Oommen, 1975, and K. N. Raj, 1975).

Furthermore, land redistribution has usually been represented to policymakers as a zero-sum, or even a negative-sum game. Total production might decline or remain the same, while the interests of the powerful few are offset against those of the numerous weak. The evidence linking redistribution of wealth and income to fertility change strongly suggests that it is not a zero-sum game. As the severity of population problems increase, the benefits of reform also increase. As policymakers are confronted with intransigent problems of underemployment, rapid urbanization, unmet needs, slowly growing per capita incomes, and rapidly growing population, they place increasing weight on policy options which have the effect of reducing fertility. Governmental actions which would have seemed unrealistically radical in the past are given serious consideration now. Fertility decline, creation of employment, and efficient use of land and labor resources are all increasingly powerful arguments in favor of land redistribution. In the words of a World Bank study (Chenery and coauthors, 1974, page 61), "In many LDC's (less developed countries) the necessary legislation (for land reform) is already in the statute books; what remains is for a ruling coalition of interests to perceive that they will gain much and lose little by implementing it." More rapid growth of income per capita and reduced population growth are strong inducements.

The final, and most compelling argument for land redistribution as an instrument of income redistribution, at least in rural areas, is that land reform is so central and highly complementary to other possible policies that, without a land reform, other policies may be ineffective or make matters even worse.

The primary alternative to a redistribution of assets in rural areas, as a means toward income redistribution and the alleviation of poverty, has been the stimulation of employment through both macroeconomic policies and large-scale rural works programs. As will be discussed in chapter 6, the world's poor are overwhelmingly dependent on wage labor for *additional* income and are faced with labor-surplus conditions where they work, so that only the provision of additional employment opportunities for unskilled and semiskilled labor can effectively raise the incomes of those at the bottom. At the macroeconomic level, the appropriate policies include the elimination of factor price distortions which encourage capital-labor substitution, shifts from protection of import-competing industries to stimulation of labor-intensive exports, changes in the internal sectoral mix of investments, and the promotion of appropriate technological choices. Empirical simulations have shown that such macroeconomic policies are moderately successful in reducing poverty and equalizing incomes (Adelman and Robinson, 1978).

Korea illustrates both the potentials and the limitations of this approach. Extremely rapid, labor-intensive outward-looking growth in Korea was apparently just able to sustain the degree of equality established earlier through asset redistribution. There are at least two important limitations to this approach. First, the base of industrial employment, especially in low-income developing countries, is small relative to the total work force, most of which remains in the traditional sector. Consequently, even if an appropriate policy framework can be established, an extremely rapid growth rate must be maintained to absorb the increase in the total labor force and to cut into preexisting labor surpluses. Realistically, employment increases must be general throughout traditional and modern sectors if the demand for labor is to outpace the supply. This general increase is almost impossible to achieve if the large majority of the population in agriculture is operating at very low marginal productivities of labor on their own holdings, while capital is being substituted for labor on large holdings. Under these circumstances, land redistribution can powerfully stimulate employment, because the labor input per cropped acre is inevitably much higher on smaller holdings. This is because of the institutional constraints on the use of purchased inputs, and also because of the fact that the intensity of use of *all* inputs together —reflecting a more intensive use of land—is higher on small holdings.

Another factor limiting employment creation through both macroeconomic policies and special work programs is the constraint on the supply of additional foodstuffs. Low-income households spend a large percentage of additional income on basic foods, mainly cereals. However, the consumption of upper- and upper-middle-income households varies little, if at all, with variations in income. This implies that income redistribution in favor of the poor would result in a large net increase in the aggregate demand for basic foods. At the same time, the price elasticities of supply of basic cereals are generally quite low, especially in the short run. This implies that a substantial rise in the money incomes of the poor, in these circumstances, cannot be translated into an increase in real income. Much will be dissipated in rising food prices, the burden of which falls on the poor and the benefits of which accrue mainly to owners of land. Under labor-surplus conditions, employment is limited by the supply of wage goods.

Land redistribution obviously relieves this constraint, because in a pattern of relatively equal smallholdings, a much larger acreage would be planted to subsistence crops. Employment increases through land redistribution are automatically accompanied by increases in the supply of basic foodstuffs. Whether the price elasticity of the marketed surplus would also increase in order to accommodate off-farm employment increases is an issue more complex, and basically empirical in nature.

Employment creation through massive rural works programs faces another set of limitations, also closely bound up with the tenurial structure. It is often overlooked that the works constructed will provide location-specific benefits mostly for landowners in the vicinity. Studies have shown that rural works construction has benefited landowners over those directly or indirectly gaining employment in the ratio of 3:1 to 5:1 (Thomas and coauthors, 1975, page 63). As a result, such programs have a much stronger impact on the distribution of income and on the extent of poverty if land is held in an unconcentrated pattern.

It is natural that landowners will be the main beneficiaries of works programs which improve the productivity and value of land. Beyond this, since landowners, along with merchants, local officials, and politicians form part of the rural elite, they are able to exert influence over project selection and implementation and thereby increase the benefits to themselves. Studies of several countries' experiences with rural works programs that were intended originally to benefit primarily the rural poor have shown that over time there is a strong tendency for these intentions to be eroded by increasing corruption, changes in the mix and location of projects, and reductions in the labor-intensity of construction technique (Srinavasan, 1974, page 374; and Thomas and coauthors, 1975, page 72). For essentially these reasons, the World Bank study (Chenery and coauthors, 1974, page 122) on distribution and development concludes, "However, in countries where the distribution of land is very skewed, a land reform makes it much easier to devise opportunities for productive investment in which benefits occur mainly to the poor. . . . Without a land reform, leakages (to nontarget groups) are likely to be large for such forms of investment as large and small-scale irrigation; other forms of land improvement such as consolidation of holdings, bunding, terracing and levelling; and investment in infrastructure, feeder roads, improved marketing facilities; clinics; clean water supplies to the village, and the like."

The possibilities for influencing wages rather than employment are limited, especially in the large, unorganized labor market. Government action can affect only money, not real wages in the long run, and only at the cost of employment expansion in the economy as a whole. Price policies are also limited in effect. Attempts to restrain the price of essential foods as a welfare measure constitute the most important of such policies for low-income groups in the short run. In Sri Lanka, for example, the free rice ration has been estimated to have had a short-run impact on the Gini coefficient of household income inequality of 6 percent, from .37 to .35 (Karuntilake, 1975). However, attempts to control commodity prices directly create the need for rationing devices of one sort or another, and it has been found almost universally that these come to operate for the benefit of the more powerful and influential groups in the economy. In India, for example, it has been found that price controls or sales below cost from the public sector of a long list if items have had a regressive impact on income distribution over a period of years. These include foreign exchange, domestic bank credit, rationed food grains, irrigation water, electric power, public housing, educational expenses, iron and steel, coal, rail transport, and other commodities (Srinavasan, 1974, pages 385–389). Price controls create implicit rents which go to influential intermediaries in the allocative process, or the low prices necessitate rationing devices which are manipulated by the more influential groups within the community to capture a disproportionate share of the scarce items, or both. It has often been found that lower-income households and smaller producers would fare better by purchasing and selling on a competitive market than they do under rationing or in markets that are ostensibly regulated for their benefit.

Many of those who doubt the feasibility of a large-scale redistribution of existing physical assets pin their hopes on a gradual redistribution of human capital stocks through an educational policy. The essence of such a policy would be public spending on primary and out-of-school educational programs designed for the mass of the population, curtailment of enrollment increases in public institutions of secondary and higher education, and a system of educational financing which subsidizes lower levels of education heavily, and relies largely on user charges to pay for the costs of higher education. This is a fair description of the South Korean educational policies discussed in chapter 4. The long-run consequences of such a policy would be a reduction in differentials in human capital financed by heavier financial burdens on the well-to-do.

In favorable cases, where the public sector represents a large segment of total output, and where the demand for public services on the part of the poorer households is strong, redistribution through public services can favorably influence the distribution of income. In Kerala and in West Malaysia, for example, this seems to have happened (Meerman, 1977; and Ratcliffe, 1977). There are strong complementarities, however, between the effects of public sector programs and the underlying distribution of income and wealth.

The data from Matar Taluka provide insight into the reasons why a policy of redistribution through education might not have a powerful effect. Tables 5-4 and 5-7 imply that in this part of rural Gujerat, educational differentials contribute little to the explanation of existing disparities. In the first place, there are few educational disparities. Almost three-quarters of adult males had no schooling; and of those who had been educated, over 90 percent had no secondary schooling. In other words, the distribution of the educational capital stock was quite egalitarian: few persons had any. The inevitable consequence of an expansion of school enrollment, such as the one which has taken place in the last decade, must be a temporary increase in the dispersion of educational attainments within the adult population. Since it is by-and-large only the children who get any schooling, and since the children become a growing minority of educated young workers as they reach maturity, the inequality in educational attainment necessarily increases until the older generation of unschooled workers is largely replaced. Therefore, over the intermediate term, an expansion of school enrollment, even if concentrated in the primary grades, will contribute to increasing inequality in most parts of rural India.

Educational attainment by itself is apparently only weakly related to higher income in rural India. This may be because the curriculum and quality of instruction in rural schools do not result in higher performance or productivity of former students in later life. This is plausible in view of the poor quality of most rural schools, especially since most students attend school for a few years only, and there are few opportunities for continuing education in the rural areas. Possibly, the only value of education is that it prepares students through training or certification for jobs outside the traditional sector, so that those who remain receive few benefits from their school attendance. In either case, any income effects of primary schooling manifest themselves with a long average lag, so that the short-run impact is insignificant. According to an International Labour Organisation (1974, page 330) study of growth and redistribution possibilities in the Philippines, "As a method of equalizing incomes, educational expansion works so slowly that even two or three decades would hardly suffice to make a dramatic difference to aggregate data on income distribution."

There are strong complementarities between the possession of physical wealth and the acquisition of human capital, and these may make it extremely difficult to use education as a redistributive mechanism without a redistribution of wealth. The returns of education are strongly dependent on family background, wealth, and land ownership. Education has more value for a future landholder than for a future agricultural laborer. The wealthier the family, the more easily will the educated urban youth find a suitable job, perhaps in another place; also, the more easily will he or she take the next step up the educational ladder.

Not only are children from better-off families able to benefit more from their education, they are also more readily provided with educational opportunities. Even without tuition or other fees, there are other indirect and opportunity costs involved in maintaining a child in school. For poor families, in which all household members must work for survival, these costs cannot readily be accepted. Consequently, even where primary school is theoretically free, school-enrollment rates are much higher for children of higher-income families. In rural West Bengal, for example, school-enrollment rates for persons aged six to fourteen rise dramatically from 22 percent for families in the lowest-expenditure decile to 76 percent for families in the highest decile (Maitra and Bhattacharya, 1974, pages 534–535). Consequently, the distribution of school attainment is likely to become more unequally distributed, the more unequal the distribution of wealth. For this reason, without an equalization of wealth, it is unlikely that education can act as a significant equalizing device.

This reasoning omits the effects of public policy on the distribution of educational benefits and costs. To the extent that education serves as a screening device for assorting new entrants into the labor force among available high-status and low-status jobs, it is likely to operate to the benefit of the children of the existing elite as a mechanism by which the elite perpetuates itself. The structure of educational costs and admissions is likely to result in a large preponderance of upper-class children in those levels and branches of education which serve as channels for entrance into the most desirable jobs. Also, these levels of education are likely to be the most heavily subsidized (Bhagwati, 1973; and Edwards and Todaro, 1974). As existing educational barriers to these positions are overcome, through a gradual rise in the numbers of persons having these qualifications, the qualifications for particular jobs will tend to be inflated in order to create new rationing devices. Under these circumstances, education is unlikely to serve any beneficial redistributive role, and, indeed, may play a perverse role. This has evidently been the case in India over the period of planning. According to Dasgupta (1974, page 70), "We also understand that government policies on educational expenditures and taxes could have been used to make the economy move toward an egalitarian society by counteracting the disequalizing forces inherent in the private sector. However, the policies which were actually adopted . . . in fact were instrumental in deteriorating the distribution of income further. Education, along with other factors, was made to serve as a disequalizer of income."

Evidently, there are strong complementarities between policies of wealth redistribution and policies of human capital redistribution through education. Lessening of disparities in wealth would make attempts to use educational policy as an instrument of income redistribution much more effective.

These complementarities may also work in the other direction as well. An educated peasantry may be more readily organized into groups able to promote and participate in cooperatives and agencies of land reform and development at the local level. In several countries organizations of small farmers and landless laborers have been important in ensuring the successful implementation of land reform (Chenery and coauthors, 1974, page 134). Basic education may facilitate the combination of peasants into such organizations and broaden their political awareness.

The general conclusion is that a redistribution of wealth is a key element in a successful policy of income redistribution. For the majority of the world's poor households who live in rural areas, this means a redistribution of land. A redistribution of tenurial rights would in itself imply a substantial increase in security. Beyond this, it would do much to assure the effectiveness of the wide range of other policy approaches to the problems of poverty and inequality. Employment-creating rural works programs are all more likely to succeed in societies without great inequalities in land ownership or in other forms of tangible wealth. There are substantial complementarities among these various approaches which operate through both economic and political mechanisms. Consequently, a combination of policies seems more likely to succeed, and land reform seems to be a critical element in such a package.

REFERENCES

Abdel-Fahid, Mahmoud. 1975. *Development, Income Distribution and Social Change in Rural Egypt, 1952–1970* (Cambridge, England, Cambridge University Press).

Abel, Martin. 1975. "The Distribution of Agricultural Development Gains in India: Case Study for South and Southeast Asia," in E. O. Heady and L. R. Whiting, eds., *Externalities in the Transformation of Agriculture* (Ames, Iowa, Iowa State University Press).

Adelman, Irma, and C. T. Morris. 1967. *Society, Politics, and Economic Development* (Baltimore, Md., The Johns Hopkins University Press).

————, and Sherman Robinson. 1978. *Income Distribution Policy in Developing Countries* (Palo Alto, Calif., Stanford University Press).

Ahluwalia, Montek. 1976. "Income Distribution and Development: Some Stylized Facts," *American Economic Review Papers and Proceedings* vol. 66, no. 2 (May) pp. 128–135.

Alamgir, Mohuiddin. 1975. "Poverty, Inequality, and Social Welfare: Measurement, Evidence, and Policy," *Bangla Desh Development Studies* vol. 3, no. 2 (April) pp. 153–180.

Bardhan, P. K. 1974. "The Pattern of Income Distribution in India," in P. K. Bardhan and T. N. Srinavasan, eds., *Poverty and Income Distribution in India* (Calcutta, Statistical Publishing Society).

Bhagwati, Jagdish. 1973. "Education, Class Structure, and Income Equality," *World Development* vol. 1, no. 5 (May) pp. 21–36.

————, and T. N. Srinavasan. 1974. *Foreign Trade Regimes and Economic Development,* vol. 6, *India* (Washington, D.C., National Bureau for Economic Research).

Bhalla, G. S. 1974. "Income Distribution Among Cultivators in Haryana: Impact of the Green Revolution," in J. C. Sandesara, ed., *The Indian Economy: Performance and Prospects* (Bombay, University of Bombay).

Byres, T. J. 1974. "Land Reform, Industrialization, and the Marketed Surplus in India: An Essay on the Power of Rural Bias," in David Lehmann, ed., *Peasants, Landlords, and Government* (New York, Holmes and Meier).

Cassen, Robert. 1975. "Welfare and Population: Notes on Rural India Since 1960," *Population and Development Review* vol. 1, no. 1 (September) pp. 33–70.

Chaudri, D. P. 1974. "New Technologies and Income Distribution in Agriculture," in David Lehmann, ed., *Peasants, Landlords and Government* (New York, Holmes and Meier).

Chenery, Hollis, Montek S. Ahluwalia, C. L. G. Bell, John H. Duloy, and Richard Jolly. 1974. *Redistribution with Growth* (Oxford, England, Oxford University Press for the World Bank and the Institute of Development Studies).

Dandekar, V. M. and N. R. Rath. 1971. "Poverty in India," *Economic and Political Weekly* (January 2).

————, and ————. 1971. "Right to Gainful Work," in P. K. Bardhan, and T. N. Srinavasan, eds., *Poverty and Income Distribution in India* (Calcutta, Statistical Publishing Society).

Dantwala, M. L., and C. H. Shah. 1971. *Evaluation of Land Reform,* vol. 2 (Bombay, U.S. Agency for International Development).

Dasgupta, A. K. 1974. "Income Distribution, Education and Capital Accumulations" (Washington, D.C., Development Research Center, International Bank for Reconstruction and Development).

Deolalikar, Anil. 1975. "Poverty and Income Distribution in an Indian Taluka" (Cambridge, Mass., Center for Population Studies, Harvard University).

————. 1977. "Returns to Scale, Factor Prices, and Small Farms in Indian Agriculture" (Senior honors thesis, Department of Economics, Harvard University).

Economic and Political Weekly. vol. 10, no. 38 (September 20, 1975).

Edwards, Edgar O., ed. 1974. *Employment in Developing Nations* (New York, Columbia University Press).

————, and Michael Todaro. 1974. "Education and Employment in Developing Nations," in E. O. Edwards, ed., *Employment in Developing Nations* (New York, Columbia University Press).

Epstein, Scarlett. 1973. *South India: Yesterday, Today, and Tomorrow* (London, Holmes and Meier).

Frankel, Francine. 1971. *India's Green Revolution: Economic Gains and Political Costs* (Princeton, N.J., Princeton University Press).

Gopinath, C., S. Krishamoorthy, and R. K. Sampath. 1977. *Land Distribution in India: Its Nature and Economic Implications* (Cambridge, Mass., Harvard Center for Population Studies).

Griffin, Keith. 1974a. *The Political Economy of Agrarian Change* (Cambridge, Mass., Harvard University Press).

————. 1974b. "Rural Development: The Policy Options," in E. O. Edwards, ed., *Employment in Developing Nations* (New York, Columbia University Press).

Griffin, Keith. 1975. "Income Inequality and Land Redistribution in Morocco," *Bangla Desh Development Studies* vol. 3, no. 3 (July) pp. 319–348.

Hanumantha Rao, C. H. 1975. *Technological Change and the Distribution of Gains in Indian Agriculture* (New Delhi, McMillan).

International Labour Organisation. 1974. *Sharing in Development: A Programme of Employment, Equity and Growth for the Philippines* (Geneva, ILO).

Joshi, P. C. 1975. *Land Reforms in India* (Delhi, Allied Publishers).

Karuntilake, Neville S. 1975. "Changes in Income Distribution in Sri Lanka," in *Income Distribution, Employment and Economic Development in East and Southeast Asia,* vol. 2 (Tokyo, Japan Economic Research Center) pp. 701–741.

Kumar, Dharma. 1974. "Changes in Income Distribution and Poverty in India: A Review of the Literature," *World Development* vol. 2, no. 1 (January) pp. 31–41.

Kuznets, Simon. 1963. "Quantitative Aspects of the Economic Growth of

Nations: III, Distribution of Income by Size," *Economic Development and Cultural Change* vol. 2 (January) pp. 1–80.

Ladejinsky, Wolf. 1973. "How Green is the Green Revolution?" *Economic and Political Weekly* (December) pp. A133–A143.

Lippitt, Victor D. 1974. *Land Reform and Economic Development in China* (New York, International Arts and Sciences).

Maitra, T., and B. D. N. Bhattacharya. 1974. "Enquiry into the Distribution of Public Education and Health Services in West Bengal," in P. K. Bardhan and T. N. Srinavasan, eds., *Poverty and Income Distribution in India* (Calcutta, Statistical Publishing Society).

Meerman, Jacob. 1977. "Meeting Basic Needs in Malaysia: A Summary of Findings" (Washington, D.C., International Bank for Reconstruction and Development).

Minhas, B. S. 1970. "Rural Poverty, Land Redistribution and Development Strategy," *Indian Economic Review* vol. 5 (April) pp. 97–128.

Mueller, Eva. 1976. "The Economic Value of Children in Peasant Agriculture," in Ronald G. Ridker, ed., *Population and Development: The Search for Selective Interventions* (Baltimore, Md., The Johns Hopkins University Press for Resources for the Future).

Mukherjee, Ramkrishna. 1971. *Six Villages of Bengal* (Bombay, Bombay Popular Prakashan).

Oommen, T. K. 1975. "Agrarian Legislation and Movements as Sources of Change: The Case of Kerala," *Economic and Political Weekly* vol. 10, no. 40 (October) pp. 1571–1583.

Pathak, R. P., K. R. Ganapathy, and Y. V. K. Sarma. 1977. "Shifts in Patterns of Assetholdings of Rural Households," *Economic and Political Weekly* (March 19) vol. 12, no. 1.

Raj, Krishna. 1975. "Measurement of the Direct and Indirect Employment Effects of Agricultural Growth with Technical Change," in L. G. Reynolds, ed., *Agriculture in Development Theory* (New Haven, Conn., Yale University Press).

Raj, K. N. 1975. "Land Reforms and Their Effect on the Distribution of Income from Land," in *Poverty, Unemployment and Development Policy*, vol. 1 (Trivandrum, Kerala, Center for Development Studies).

Ratcliffe, John. 1977. "Poverty, Politics, and Fertility: The Anomaly of Kerala," *The Hastings Center Report* vol. 7, no. 1 (February).

Rosenzweig, M. R., and R. Evenson. 1976. "Fertility, Schooling, and the Economic Contribution of Children in Rural India." Paper presented at the annual Meeting of the Population Association of America, Montreal, April.

Sanpath, R. K. 1975. "Inter-regional Inequality in India, 1951–1971" (Cambridge, Mass., Harvard University Center for Population Studies).

Sen, A. K. 1974. "Poverty, Inequality and Unemployment: Some Conceptual

Issues in Measurement," in P. K. Bardhan and T. N. Srinavasan, eds., *Poverty and Income Distribution in India* (Calcutta, Statistical Publishing Society).

Shah, Vimal, and R. Repetto. 1975. "Demographic and Other Influences on Long-Term Savings Behavior in a Rural Development Block in India" (Cambridge, Mass., Harvard Center for Population Studies).

Shah, Vimal, and C. H. Shah. 1974. *Resurvey of Matar Taluka* (Bombay, Vora Publishers).

Simon, Julian. 1972. "The Effects of Income Redistribution on Fertility in Less-developed Countries" (Washington, D.C., U.S. Department of State).

Simon, Julian. 1974. *The Effects of Income on Fertility* (Chapel Hill, N.C., Carolina Population Center).

Srinavasan, T. N. 1974. "Income Distribution: A Survey of Policy Aspects," in P. K. Bardhan and T. N. Srinavasan, eds., *Poverty and Income Distribution in India* (Calcutta, Statistical Publishing Society).

Thomas, John W., Richard Hook, Javed Burki, and David Davies. 1975. *Public Works Programs in Developing Countries: A Comparative Analysis* (Cambridge, Mass., Harvard Institute for International Development).

Timur, Serim. 1971. "Socio-Economic Correlates of Differential Fertility in Turkey." Paper submitted to the Second Europe Population Conference, Strasbourg, August/September.

Vaidyanathan, A. 1974. "Some Aspects of Inequalities in Living Standards in Rural India," in P. K. Bardhan and T. N. Srinavasan, eds., *Poverty and Income Distribution in India* (Calcutta, Statistical Publishing Society).

Warriner, Doreen. 1969. *Land Reform in Principle and Practice* (Oxford, England, Oxford University Press).

6 |「┎ INTERNATIONAL IMPLICATIONS

The world fertility rate is affected by the international distribution of income in the same way that national fertility rates are affected by income distributions within countries. The same reasoning and kinds of evidence used in interpreting national fertility rates are applicable to the world rate, and lead to an analogous conclusion: a more equal distribution of income among countries would be conducive to a lower global birth rate and a lower rate of world population growth.

This conclusion follows almost immediately from the facts of the present world demographic situation. They are such that future changes in fertility rates in the rich countries can have little influence over the course of the global birth rate or global population growth. These depend much more heavily on future changes in birth rates in the poor countries. Consequently, the impact of economic growth on fertility and the pace of economic growth in the rich countries are largely irrelevant to the pace of world population change. Whatever the income-fertility link is in the rich countries, it is relatively unimportant from the global perspective. What is important is the fertility decline in the poor countries, and if economic growth is conducive to that decline, then, from the standpoint of world population growth, only economic development in the poor countries really matters.

The people of the developed countries constitute a small minority in the world, and contribute an even smaller minority of all births. In 1970, only about 30 percent of the world's population lived in what are conventionally classified as the developed countries (UN, 1974, page 5). Irrespective of future changes in vital rates, this percentage will inevitably shrink for some time to come, by virtue of the younger age structure in the less-developed countries. Further, in 1970, the 30 percent of the world's population living in the rich countries generated only 16 percent of all births.

In the developed countries fertility, already low, is near replacement level, and is unlikely to change very much in the future. It is unlikely to fall much below replacement levels for sustained periods of time. At the same time, fertility rates are unlikely to reverse themselves and return to anything like the levels from which they have declined in the developed countries. Fertility norms in the developed countries are apparently converging and stabilizing around the two-child family. The whole process of urbanization, industrialization, and improved communications, health conditions, and opportunities for women, and the better control over fertility are unlikely to be reversed in the relevant future. In addition, the relatively flat age distribution in the developed countries implies that coming cohorts of child-bearing women will be only moderately larger than the present one. The fact that fertility has been low for some time in the developed countries means that the coming generation is not of a size which creates great momentum for future growth.

In the poor countries, by contrast, the age structure is strongly pyramidal, future cohorts of women will be substantially larger than at present; and, therefore, the future fertility rates of these cohorts will be extremely significant. Although both fertility and the rate of population growth are declining in the less-developed countries, they are both high. In 1974 the crude birth rate for the less-developed countries was 35 to 37 per 1,000, and the crude death rate was 13 to 14. The latter might yet fall by another 50 percent, because of the young age of the population. Even though declines in the present high birth rates have begun in a number of countries, the age structure remains sharply pyramidal. Therefore, a great deal of additional population growth will take place before ultimate stabilization occurs.

The implications of these demographic facts have been demonstrated in a set of projections set forth by Frejka (1974). Using a standard, plausible assumption about the pace of future declines in mortality rates and alternative projections of the decline in fertility rates to replacement levels, Frejka made projections of worldwide population growth, and for the developed and less-developed regions separately. The alternative projections of fertility trends assume linear declines in the net reproduction rate to replacement level in periods of zero, ten, thirty, fifty, and seventy years. The results are striking. For the developed countries, the difference between the fastest and slowest fertility decline, in terms of total population, is only 125 million people by the year 2000 and 525 million by the year 2100. For the less-developed countries, the difference by the year 2000 is 2,729 million. This is over twenty times as large as the difference made by the same alternative fertility assumptions for the developed countries. For the year 2100, the difference between the most optimistic and pessimistic assumptions, in terms of total population, is 9,612 million. In other words, whatever happens to fertility in the rich countries, world population growth is going to be overwhelmingly influenced by what happens in the poor countries. Moreover, world population will be greatly influenced by what happens in the developing countries in the near future. According to Frejka (1974, page 176), "One implication of the above findings cannot be stressed enough: long-term population growth of the LDC's depends heavily on fertility changes of the near future. This is so because current high fertility is producing large stocks of future child bearers."

There is also abundant evidence that income growth in the developed countries is likely to have little net impact on their birth rates. The primary reason for this is that within the developed countries, almost all subgroups have converged to a similar pattern of low fertility. Modern attitudes, contraceptive knowledge, and the opportunities and constraints of modern life are already sufficiently widespread so that a large proportion of households in the developed countries have been affected and have lowered their fertility accordingly (Freedman, 1960, page 74; and Ryder, 1973, page 65).

This is evident in the narrowing of fertility differentials by socioeconomic category in the developed countries since World War II. Fertility differentials, which had arisen and persisted or widened in the nineteenth and early twentieth centuries, have narrowed and largely disappeared since 1945. In Europe, various differentials had narrowed or become erratic, even by 1960 (Johnson, 1960, page 36). By 1970 they had converged to such a degree that a leading European demographer (Tabah, 1971, page 140) could write as follows:

Over the past century fertility in Western Europe has been steadily declining, and seems to be converging within a fairly slender bracket of between 2.3 to 2.7 births per woman among the generation reaching the reproductive age, immediately after the war, declining still further in the most recent further generations. The situation appears to be growing more homogenous, in terms of space, time, and the social hierarchy, as though the family were approaching a model, standard pattern. . . . Differences among countries, regions, and social classes have lessened to such an extent that it seems useless to discus them unless we wish to split hairs.

In the United States, fertility differentials narrowed during the baby boom of the early 1950s, as those groups with the lowest fertility in population experienced the largest percentage increases (Kiser, 1960). Since 1957, in a period of substantial fertility decline, differentials have narrowed still further, or disappeared altogether. Furthermore, differentials in desired fertility are even narrower than those of attained fertility, and much of the more rapid fall in the birth rates of high-fertility groups has been caused by the elimination of unwanted fertility through more widespread and efficient contraception. This process of convergence in the period of recent fertility decline has been characterized by Sweet (1974, page 107) in the following way: "The continuous decline in fertility in the U.S. since 1957, while affecting all elements of the population, has been most pronounced and most rapid among those groups which previously had the highest fertility—blacks, American Indians, and Mexican Americans—all of whom experienced fertility declines greater than those experienced by urban whites between 1957–60 and 1967–70. Among urban whites, fertility decline has been heavily concentrated among those of low income. The decline was especially rapid for third and higher-order births, suggesting a heavy concentration of completed fertility at two-child families."

The narrowing or elimination of socioeconomic differentials in fertility, and the convergence of desired and actual family size to a low level, implying little more than replacement, is evidently widespread or nearly universal throughout the developed world. In addition to the experience of Europe and America, it seems to be the emerging pattern in Japan, for example (Hashimoto, 1974). As this process is completed, further economic growth will have the effect, not of driving the demographic transition to completion, but of shifting the entire fertility schedule, of all groups and classes within the population, up or down. Such shifts may be small, for several reasons.

The advanced countries' populations show the characteristic U-shaped pattern of fertility at different income levels. At high-income levels, fertility tends to be somewhat higher than at middle-income levels (Bogue, 1969; Simon, 1974; and Tabah, 1971). This may be indicative of a reversal or weakening of the inverse effect of income on fertility as

Table 6-1. Test of Nonlinearity in the Influence of Income per Capita on Fertility Rates Across Countries: Cross-national Regressions of the Gross Reproduction Rate on Selected Socioeconomic Variables

Dependent variable GRR, 1965–70	Constant term	Income per capita squared (in hundreds of U.S.$)	Income per capita (in hundreds of U.S.$)	Gini coefficient of income concentration	Infant mortality rate	Female literacy rate	R^2
Regression 1	3.37	−.227	.0000545				.64
(t-ratio)		(−8.3)	(5.2)				
Partial correlation with gross reproduction rate		−.72	5.4				
Regression 2	2.33	−.201	.0000490	2.11			.70
(t-ratio)		(−7.6)	(4.9)	(3.4)			
Partial correlation with gross reproduction rate		−.64	.39	.39			
Regression 3	2.46	−.132	.000011	1.96	.00066	−.727	.75
(t ratio)		(−4.1)	(3.1)	(3.4)	(0.4)	(−2.1)	
Partial correlation with gross reproduction rate		−.46	.36	.39	.05	−.26	

Note: For a definition of the variables and an explanation of data source, see chapter 2.

income levels rise. Also, econometric studies of fertility in developed countries demonstrate that the net effect of income changes is a balance between a positive-wealth effect and a negative-substitution effect (Schultz, 1974; and Simon, 1974), and that this net effect tends to be small. Further, the effect of improved economic conditions on nuptiality may be offsetting to their impact on marital fertility: improved economic conditions may induce earlier and more universal marriage and family formation, offsetting any net negative effect on marital fertility. Consequently, the net effect of further economic growth on the overall fertility rates of rich countries will be small and perhaps positive.

This suggests that the relationship between income growth and fertility should change for countries as they pass through various ranges of per capita income. For countries embarked on the demographic transition, economic growth—which, speaking broadly, extends modernity throughout the population—should result in substantial fertility declines. For countries in which modernity and its characteristic fertility and contraceptive behavior have already been widely diffused, economic growth should result in small declines, or even, possibly, increases in fertility. In other words, the same pattern of nonlinearity which is evident among households at different income levels within countries should also be found in comparisons of entire countries at different income levels. The characteristic U-shaped relationship of fertility to per capita income should be found in cross-national comparisons, as well.

The hypothesis was readily tested with the use of the cross-national sample of sixty-eight countries that had been used previously in analyzing the effects of intracountry income distribution. The procedure simply involved a test for nonlinearity of the relationship of fertility, measured by the gross reproduction rate, to mean per capita income in each country. Nonlinearity was tested by the coefficient of a quadratic term in mean per capita income in the regression of fertility on a list of explanatory variables across the sample of sixty-eight countries. No significance is attached to this particular functional form. It is merely a second-order approximation to the underlying function and is useful only for the testing of an hypothesis. In view of the possible crudeness of the data and the simplicity of the argument, ordinary least-squares estimates were computed. The possibility and direction of biases from this procedure in the estimates were discussed in chapter 2. The results are presented in table 6-1.

It is clear from the statistics presented in columns three and four of table 6-1 that the hypothesis of linearity is decisively rejected. The

Table 6-2.   The Estimated Marginal Effect of an Increase
of $100 in Mean Per Capita Income on the Gross
Reproduction Rate, for Countries at Various Levels
of Average Per Capita Income

Average per capita income level	Effect on the gross reproduction rate of a rise of $100 in average per capita income
$100	−.22
$200	−.20
$500	−.17
$1000	−.12
$1500	−.06
$2000	−.01
$3000	+.10

Source: Computed from regression equation 1 in
table 6-1.

relationship of fertility to per capita income is strongly U-shaped across
the sample of sixty-eight developed and less-developed countries. The
nonlinear term in per capita income for each regression is significantly
different from zero, whatever the list of additional explanatory variables.
The linear term is invariably negative. The gross reproduction rate reaches
a minimum with respect to mean income per capita at an income level of
about $2,000 in 1964 U.S. dollars. The marginal effect of income changes
on fertility rises substantially in absolute terms, as table 6-2 indicates.
While the estimated impact on the gross reproduction rate of an increase
of $100 in annual per capita income is −.2 at the $200 per capita income
level, it is only −.06 at the $1,500 per capita income level.

The extent of nonlinearity, as revealed in table 6-3—as well as the
size of the partial correlation coefficients of the income per capita variables in the regressions of table 6-2—point up the importance of the international distribution of income along with the internal distribution of
income in determining birth rates. The two distributional variables, internal and international, are more closely related to fertility than are the
infant mortality rate or the female literacy rate, although these two are
by far the more frequently considered as areas of importance in the design
of population policies. The evidence presented above supports the contention that population policies which concerned themselves with the
pattern of income growth and distribution, both within and among countries, would have a greater impact than those which did not.

Table 6-3. Estimated Demographic Significance of Income Growth in Developed and Less-Developed Countries, 1960–70

	More-developed countries	Less-developed countries	Share of less-developed countries
Population, 1960[a]	976 mil.	2,019 mil.	.67
Population, 1970[a]	1,084 mil.	2,547 mil.	.70
Crude birth rate, 1960[a]	21.1	41.0	
Crude birth rate, 1970[a]	17.6	38.5	
No. of births, 1970	19.1 mil.	98.1 mil.	.84
No. of births, 1970 at 1960 crude birth rate	22.9 mil.	104.4 mil.	
Difference in no. of births	3.8 mil.	6.3 mil.	.62
GNP, 1970 in billions of U.S.$[b]	2,664	555	.17
Percentage increase in 1960–70 constant prices[c]	63	74	
Increase in GNP, 1960–70, in billions of U.S.$ constant prices	1,030	236	.19
Incremental ratio of GNP growth to fertility decline, 1960–70	$27,100	$3,750	

Sources:

[a] United Nations, *The Population Debate: Materials and Perspectives* (New York, UN, 1970) p. 5; p. 207; 1970 crude birth rates have been interpolated from estimates for 1965–70 and 1970–75.

[b] U.S. Department of Commerce, *Statistical Abstract of the U.S.* (Washington, D.C., 1973) p. 813.

[c] U.S. Department of State, Agency for International Development, *Growth Rate and Trend Data*, (Washington, D.C., USAID, May 1, 1974).

From the standpoint of rapid fertility decline and stabilization of the world's population, the pattern of income growth in the world during the past decades has been clearly inappropriate. The overwhelming bulk of income growth has taken place in the already rich countries, where it is demographically ineffective. Table 6-3 illustrates this phenomenon with some crude summary statistics for the period 1960–70. In 1970, the less-developed countries, which had 70 percent of the world's population and generated 84 percent of the world's births, received only 17 percent of the world's income. Moreover, between 1960–70, only 19 percent of the growth in world income accrued to the less-developed countries, while 81 percent accrued to the already developed regions.

An indication of the demographic effectiveness of these increments to income in rich and poor countries has been calculated by estimating the declines in fertility in rich and poor countries and comparing these to the increments to income. The declines in fertility were roughly estimated by applying 1960 crude birth rates to 1970 population totals in each region, and subtracting from these products the actual number of births in 1970. The resulting estimates measure the difference between the actual number of births in 1970 and the numbers which would have been experienced had 1960 crude birth rates persisted in 1970. The differences are 6.3 million births per year in the less-developed countries, and 3.8 million in the advanced countries. Even though the 1960s were years in which substantial, and probably once-over declines in fertility took place in the developed countries, the much greater part of total fertility decline took place in the less-developed regions. The nonrepeatable elements in the fertility decline in the rich countries include (1) the elimination of unwanted fertility through greater contraceptive efficiency; (2) the deferral of childbearing during the late 1960s; and (3) the reduction of exceptionally high fertility rates associated with the baby boom of the late 1950s. It is unlikely that fertility in the rich countries would again fall at the rates experienced between 1960–70.

Nevertheless, comparing the declines in numbers of births in the rich and poor countries with the increases in incomes, it is clear that economic growth in the less-developed countries, in dollars per birth, has been considerably more strongly associated with fertility decline than that in the rich nations. In the rich nations, between 1960–70, there was a $27,000 rise in income per unit decline in the number of births; in the poor nations, there was a $3,750 rise in income for each unit fall in the number of births. There are severe problems involved in attempts to measure international differences in real living standards by dollar-income differentials. Exchange-rate conversions and relative price differentials result in monetary differentials which overstate real income differences, perhaps as much as a factor of two or three. Nonetheless, despite the crudeness of the methodology and data underlying this comparison, it is clear that two quite different orders of magnitude are involved. The incremental income-fertility ratio in the rich countries is seven times as high as it is in the poor countries, and this difference is likely to widen in the future.

More detailed data bear out this conclusion. Table 6-4 presents information on population and income growth between 1960–73 for countries grouped by the level of per capita income in 1973. The overwhelming bulk of income growth took place in the upper-income groups of countries which contain only a small fraction of the world's population.

This income growth was only tenuously related to fertility decline. The ratio of income growth to fertility decline was considerably lower in the poor countries than in the rich. This is a further indication of the negligible contribution that economic growth in the already developed countries can make to the overall decline in world fertility.

Table 6-6 presents another way of looking at the demographic effectiveness of income growth in the developed and less-developed countries. From the demographic standpoint, effective income growth is that which contributes to the decline in world fertility rates. Consequently, the calculated marginal impact coefficients of income growth on fertility, presented in table 6-2, can be appropriately used as weights in recomputing income growth in countries at various levels of income per capita. In low-income countries, in which economic growth has a strong inverse relation to fertility, income growth would receive a relatively high weight; in high-income countries, in which the relationship is weakly inverse, zero, or direct income growth would receive a small, zero, or negative weight. Table 6-5 presents (1) the demographic weights based on these estimated marginal impact coefficients; (2) the distribution of actual income growth in U.S. dollars between 1960–70 among countries at various levels of income per capita; and (3) the distribution of demographically effective income growth among the same countries. The differences are striking. While the bulk (86.3 percent) of the world's income growth during the 1960s took place in countries with per capita incomes above $1,000 per year, only a small percentage (4.4 percent) of demographically effective income growth took place in those developed countries. Also, while only 7.4 percent of actual income growth took place in the poor countries with per capita income below $300, as much as 59.6 percent of the demographically effective income growth took place in those less-developed regions. This is yet another way of underlining the fundamental point of this chapter; that is, it is only the economic development which takes place in the poor countries which is of significance to the solution of the problem of world population growth; that all the economic growth in the already developed countries is at best irrelevant or, at worst, competitive for scarce resources.

Yet, the problem of inequalities is evidently considerably more serious at the international level than it is within most individual countries. In spite of the difficulties in making comparisons of income levels and living standards across countries, this has been the conclusion of a number of attempts at assessment of the international distribution of income. The

Table 6-4. Growth in the Gross Domestic Product (GDP) and Decline in Births, 1960–73, by Countries at Different Incomes Per Capita

	Range of Gross Domestic Product, in U.S. $							
	0–99	100–199	200–299	300–599	600–999	1,000–1,499	1,500–2,999	3,000+
Population, 1,773 million	196.1	953.8	1,015.8	214.4	287.4	68.8	466.9	610.3
Percentage distribution of population, 1973	5.14	25.0	26.6	5.6	7.5	1.8	12.2	16.0
GDP, 1973, in billions of $	15.6	106.4	264.4	68.3	166.9	45.0	390.6	2,899.6
Percentage distribution of 1973 GDP	0.4	2.7	6.7	1.7	4.2	1.1	9.8	73.3
Growth in GDP, 1960–73, in billions of $	4.9	49.3	143.8	49.3	117.9	33.1	250.2	2,013.2
Percentage distribution of growth in GDP	0.2	1.8	5.4	1.8	4.4	1.2	9.4	75.6
No. of 1973 births, based on 1960 crude birth rates, in millions	9.27	47.67	70.02	9.33	12.96	1.81	11.12	12.88
No. of 1973 births, in millions	8.98	42.02	67.09	8.98	11.64	1.69	8.90	10.97
Estimated decline in births, in thousands	288.2	5,653.5	2,936.1	351.6	1,323.7	122.3	2,224.3	2,908.2
Growth of GDP per birth reduction, for 1960–73, in millions of $	17.2	8.7	48.9	140.27	89.07	270.7	112.5	271.2

Table 6-5. Distribution of Actual and Demographically Effective Income Growth, 1960–73, Among Countries by Level of Per Capita Income

Income per capita range ($ per year)	% of world population, 1970	Growth in GDP, 1960–73 (in millions of $)	Demographic effectiveness weights for income growth	Demographically effective income growth	% distribution of demographically effective income growth	% distribution of actual income growth
0–99	5.1	4,971	.240	1,193	1.6	.19
100–199	25.0	49,328	.228	11,246	15.2	1.85
200–299	27.0	143,844	.216	31,070	42.8	5.40
300–599	5.6	49,319	.193	9,518	12.8	1.85
600–999	7.5	117,905	.152	17,921	24.2	4.43
1,000–1,499	1.8	33,106	.098	3,244	4.4	1.24
1,500–2,999	12.2	250,218	−.019	—	—	9.40
3,000+	16.0	2,013,025	−.108	—	—	75.63

Gini coefficient of the distribution of income across countries seems to be in the range of .50 to .60, which is higher than in any of the presently developed countries, and as high as in those developing countries with the most unequal income distribution (Beckerman and Bacon, 1970, page 62; Chenery and coauthors, 1974, page 159; and King and coauthors, page 37).

That the distribution of income internationally should be more unequal than almost any national distribution is not surprising. National boundaries create significant barriers to factor mobility, and this greatly reduces a primary mechanism for the equalization of incomes across regions. Given the barriers to international trade as well, commodity flows are evidently weak substitutes for factor movements. Moreover, the political demands and institutional mechanisms for the transfer of resources to equalize living standards among households are substantially weaker across national boundaries than within them. There is both a lack of consensus and ideological commitment to the idea of international equality, and a lack of established institutional means for the large-scale transfer of resources.

Not only are international disparities large, they have been growing and continue to grow. Systematic income differentials between the presently developed and undeveloped regions have their origins in the Industrial Revolution, thus dating back less than 200 years (Bhagwati, 1972, pages 6–7). They have as much to do with the differential rates of accumulation of technical knowledge and skills as with differentials in the rate of capital accumulation. During the 1950s and 1960s, the international disparities between rich and poor nations continued to rise, partially because a far larger share of the economic advance in the less-developed countries had been offset by population growth. In the 1970s, international disparities greatly worsened, because the crisis of the first half of the decade affected most severely the poorest of the less-developed countries. As table 6-6 shows, the countries of South Asia and sub-Saharan Africa, where most of those in conditions of absolute poverty are located, grew at less than one-third the rate of all other countries.

Most, although not all, of the opportunities for changing the course of this deterioration in international income distribution are in the hands of the rich countries, simply because they are powerful and dominant. Unfortunately, these opportunities have been seen in the rich countries to have zero-sum payoff structures. Concessions to the developing countries or gains by them have been assumed to imply costs or losses to the

Table 6-6.   GNP Per Capita Growth Rates in Selected Areas, 1951–75
(% per annum)

Area	1951–60	1961–70	1971–75	1951–75
South Asia	2.7	1.5	0.5	1.8
East Asia	3.3	4.0	4.8	3.9
Sub-Saharan Africa	2.4	1.6	2.1	2.0
Middle East	5.0	4.4	6.4	5.0
Latin America	2.1	2.5	3.7	2.6
All less-developed countries	2.8	3.2	3.0	3.1
OECD countries	3.0	3.7	1.9	3.2

Source: International Bank for Reconstruction and Development, Development Policy Staff, Prospects for Developing Countries, 1978–85 (Washington, D.C., IBRD, 1977) p. 6.

developed world. As a result, international economic policy changes and North–South resource transfers have been either resisted, or manipulated to serve the rich countries' interests in ways that reduce their developmental impact.

This stance is evident in matters of trade as well as international finance. Liberalization of trade in labor-intensive manufactures of special interest to exporters in less-developed countries, and in primary commodities in processed form, has lagged behind liberalization of trade among rich countries. The gains from the expansion of international monetary reserves have benefited the rich countries most directly, and attempts to link the requirements of monetary expansion with those of capital transfers from rich to poor have been resisted. Official capital transfers remain well below modest targets, and have been eroded considerably by rising debt service requirements and costs of imports to the less-developed countries.

Yet, it is recognized that the rapid growth of world population, mainly in the less-developed countries, is a serious threat to future world stability and welfare. Based on a narrow view of the problem, Western countries have poured money into support for family-planning programs, have funded research into contraceptive techniques, and have increasingly linked support for development activities in the less-developed countries to their taking effective steps for the reduction of population growth rates.

An increase in the flow of resources to the world's poor, for whom an improvement of income prospects and conditions of life would encourage a fertility decline, is a major part of the solution to the problem of population growth. In addition to ethical considerations, the developed countries' stake in limiting the future world population growth implies a positive interest in promoting rapid socioeconomic advances among the bottom half of the income distribution in the developing countries. The most effective response of the rich countries to the challenge of rapid population growth in the world would be the adoption of international economic policies which do this. In addition, the wealthier nations should strongly support governments and policies in the less-developed countries which bring about internal changes in the distribution of income and wealth in favor of the poor.

If this course is adopted, the costs to the developed countries will not be great. The combination of great inequalities *internationally* and great inequalities *internally* within the poor countries means that the world's poor receive a strikingly small fraction of the world's income. Even after allowing for the difficulties of comparing living standards internationally, one must conclude that countries in the bottom half of the world's income distribution receive at most 10 percent. In addition, the poorest half of the population in those countries probably receives less than 20 percent of that income. In other words, the poorest one-quarter of the world's population, about 1 billion persons, receives only about 2 percent of the total world income. By similar reasoning, the poorest 40 percent of the world's population probably receives only about 5 percent of world income. Since the rich countries receive about 85 percent of world income, these percentages, in terms of their income alone, still remain in the vicinity of 3 and 6 percent, respectively. Policies which would transfer resources from the developed countries directly to the poor of the poorer countries, combining internal and international redistribution, would make major changes among the world's poor at a cost which would be minor in terms of the resources at the disposal of the developed countries.

In fact, there is evidence that internal and international redistribution may be the *only* feasible approach to the problem of raising the living standards of the world's poor to some reasonable minimal level. Simulations carried out for the UN and the International Labour Organisation, using a regional network of linked input-output models for the world's economy, indicate that even under the assumption of optimistically rapid growth in both developed and underdeveloped regions, with no redistribution, severe constraints on resource availability would be reached before minimal standards had been achieved by the world's poor. It is obvious that if the upper 90 percent of income, received by the world's rich must grow rapidly in order that the bottom 10 percent may also do so, severe limitations on resources, capital, and other inputs will be encountered (Stern, 1976). Also, policies which transfer resources to less-developed countries for distribution, as income is presently distributed, are costly and unattractive, because the rich in poor countries now secure a very large share of the available resources. In the international realm, developed countries have an interest in policies which provide additional resources directly to the world's poor.

The nature of these policies follows directly from the characteristics of the world's low-income households, and the structure of the developing economies in which most of them live. The remainder of this chapter will take up these considerations in turn.

To a very good approximation, the world's poor are dependent on wage labor for additional earnings. These households do not have appreciable capital, either physical or human. Consequently, their members earn their livings by unskilled and semiskilled labor. The main poverty groups are (1) landless agricultural laborers; (2) marginal farmers on inadequate landholdings; (3) the urban unemployed; and (4) urban casual laborers and participants in the urban informal sector. All these groups, except the marginal farmers, are obviously dependent on employment, directly or indirectly, for income increases. In the urban informal sector, returns to self-employment among petty traders and service workers are determined by the numbers unable to find regular wage employment who crowd into these occupations. Their earnings thus depend on the strength of demand for unskilled and semiskilled labor and the growth rate of wage employment. As for marginal farmers, numerous studies have shown that they derive increasing fractions of their incomes from off-farm employment as the man–land ratio rises and the marginal productivity of labor expended on small holdings diminishes. In extreme cases, 75 or 80 percent of earnings on the average among farmers in the smallest-sized holdings comes from off-farm employment. At the margin, the dependency on wage employment for incremental income is even higher. Therefore, aside from a redistribution of earning assets, which is not in the realm of international policy, the world's poor can experience rising incomes only through increases in real wage earnings.

The second important fact is that the large majority of the world's poor live in conditions of labor surplus. There is so much slack in markets for unskilled and semiskilled labor that a substantial additional work force could be drawn out of the informal sector and traditional agriculture without any increase in the real wage. The supply of labor, in other words (if not of special skills), is perfectly elastic. These conditions certainly hold in South Asia and sub-Saharan Africa, where most of the world's poor reside; but also in other regions of substantial poverty, such as rural Java, the northeastern part of Brazil, and other rural areas of Latin America. Even in small, middle-income countries which have grown rapidly, such as Korea and Taiwan, the turning point in labor markets at which real wages began systematically to increase came fairly late in the course of development (Ranis and Fei, 1975).

Labor-surplus conditions and elastic supply of labor in the poor developing countries imply that policies which raise value added per unit of output will not raise wage levels. They will raise the returns to non-labor factor inputs which are available in inelastic supply. Labor earnings will rise only from increases in output and employment. Thus, for example, policies which raise the prices of the exports of labor-surplus less-developed countries at the expense of their volume will not raise labor earnings, even though total export revenues increase. The added revenues will remain with nonlabor factors, and if output and employment decline in the export sector, labor earnings will fall.

This is a partial point of view. It might be argued that whoever receives the income will spend it, and thereby create a larger domestic demand for output and for labor. In this view, the final result is indeterminate, depending on supply and demand responses throughout the economy.

In fact, the situation is simpler than that. The third important structural characteristic of the developing countries is that the factor content of final demand is essentially the same for all income groups. The employment created by an additional unit of income spent by the rich is much the same as that created by an additional unit of income spent by the poor. This counterintuitive result has been demonstrated in a number of studies for a substantial number of developing countries (Cline, 1975; Chinn, 1977; and Morley and Williamson, 1974). The reason is, essentially, that the rich consume a great many labor-intensive services and labor-intensive products such as housing; while the poor consume many items which may be, at the margin, quite capital-intensive, such as agricultural products. Increases in agricultural output often require heavy investments in irrigation systems, fertilizer production, and so forth. Empirically, there is little difference in the employment implications of additional spending by various economic groups in the developing countries.

For this reason, in comparing alternative international economic policies affecting the world's poor, second-round and general equilibrium effects within the developing countries are unimportant. The policy which most benefits the poor directly in the form of increased employment per unit of additional income generated will also most benefit the poor ultimately. It is sufficient to determine which of alternative policies capable of accelerating income growth in the less-developed countries will lead directly to the greatest increases in employment.

Implicit in this approach is the additional assumption that domestic policy choices within the less-developed countries, with regard to institutional changes and to the distributive burden of public finance, are made independently of the international economic framework. Governments in the developing countries which wish to redistribute land or to make their revenue structures and expenditures more progressive can do so. Therefore, attention need not be focused on the impact of international economic policies on government revenues in less-developed countries. Domestic policy is separable, at least with regard to its distributive aspect.

Within this conceptual framework, it is evident which kinds of international economic policies would be more effective in providing increased incomes and employment to the world's poor (Repetto, 1978). In the commodity field there are distinct alternatives with regard to international trade policies. It is now clear that the experience of OPEC cannot be generalized to other commodities exported by less-developed countries. Primarily, this is so because there are no other commodities for which the less-developed countries command so large a market share, for which substitutes are so hard to find, and for which production is so concentrated among a small number of major producers. Even in the short run, the possibilities are limited for increasing the income of producers in less-developed countries by placing restrictions on supply through inter-country commodity agreements, although, naturally, the possibilities expand if consuming countries are willing to participate in the agreements. In the longer run, as substitution on the demand and supply sides becomes easier, the potential revenue increases to producers diminishes. Also, because for most primary commodities, low-income countries include both producers and consumers, the distributional impacts are quite mixed, even though, on balance, the low-income countries are net exporters of most primary commodities.

A distinct alternative to trade restriction as a means of increasing the incomes of primary producers is trade liberalization. Commodities such as meat, sugar, vegetables, oils, and wine, which compete with internal production in the rich countries, are subject to stringent and often absolute trade barriers in the form of quantitative restrictions. In addition, tariff escalation in the developed countries on the processed forms of almost all primary commodities restricts the value added and employment derived from primary production in less-developed countries by inhibiting processing. Often this processing, especially of agricultural, husbandry, and timber products, can be very labor-intensive. Partially in response to tariff escalation in the rich countries, the export duties from the developing countries are made higher on the crude forms than on the processed forms of primary commodities. This helps to preserve the pattern of comparative advantage, but it also restricts the volume of world trade. Studies have indicated that removal of barriers to imports in the rich countries and de-escalation of tariffs could result in a large increase in export earnings and volumes in the less-developed countries. These increases accelerate over time, as long-term supply and demand elasticities are relatively large. They are ultimately larger than those available from additional cartelization of commodity trade.

It is clear that of these two policy alternatives, laborers in developing countries would benefit most from trade liberalization and mutual reduction in tariff escalation. Cartelization of commodity trade through producer agreements reduces the volume of production and exports to achieve higher prices and revenues. However, for already obvious reasons, those additional revenues are unlikely to go to unskilled and semiskilled workers in the form of higher real wages. On the contrary, the reduced production implies lower employment and lower wage earnings. By contrast, trade liberalization increases output and employment. For the same amount of additional income accruing to the developing countries, the benefits to unskilled and semiskilled labor will be much greater. The liberal trade regime emerges as the international policy which extends the greater potential of additional income to the world's poor.

A very similar conclusion applies to the international policy toward trade in manufactured goods between less-developed and advanced countries. Despite discriminatory barriers against manufactured exports from developing countries, the international regime has been sufficiently liberal to allow rapid expansion of North–South trade in an increasing range of products. Exporting countries which have established outward-looking economic strategies have experienced unprecedented rapid growth, have attracted ample financial investment and direct investment oriented toward export production, and have established marketing channels and a valuable knowledge of international business operations. Because of specialization in labor-intensive lines of production, both productivity and employment growth have been extremely rapid. Since these export industries are intensive in relatively unskilled labor, low-income workers have been direct beneficiaries.

Especially in the most labor-intensive industries, in which exports from less-developed countries might naturally capture a very large market share in the developed countries, quantitative restrictions have provided ample protection to producers in the richer countries. The impacts of these restrictions have been softened through negotiation in order to permit specified growth rates for efforts and to enable the exporting countries to capture the rents stemming from higher export unit values voluntary export restrictions. Such agreements, however, have markedly different distributional implications within the exporting countries than would the alternative of fixed *ad valorem* tariffs.

As demand within the importing community increases, *ad valorem* tariffs permit rising export volumes and values, stimulating output and employment in the exporting countries. Also, less-developed countries can offset the tariff through devaluation, if necessary. By contrast, quantitative restrictions, including voluntary export restrictions, permit increasing export unit values but hold back the increase in export volumes. Consequently, even though the latter might result in additional export revenues for the less-developed countries, that revenue will not be passed along in the form of increased wage employment. Rather, it will be captured by monopolistic elements in the export industry or by the government, depending on the market organization. For the poor, trade policy which replaces quantitative restrictions with fixed tariffs has very favorable distributional implications over time.

This is particularly true in the case of textiles, wearing apparel, footwear, and similar simple labor-intensive manufactured goods which have been the main targets of quantitative restrictions by the advanced countries. The successful exporters of the past—Hong Kong, Singapore, Korea, Taiwan, Mexico, Brazil, and Yugoslavia—have already lost much of their comparative advantage. In this group of now middle-income countries, successful labor-intensive growth in the past has absorbed the pool of surplus labor. Wage rates and labor costs have risen, and the export mix of these economies has shifted toward a more skill-intensive and capital-intensive range of products. Truly low-wage countries with surplus labor are taking over export markets for these products. No other policy change would be of such direct and significant benefit to the world's poor as the liberalization of trade in simple labor-intensive manufactures.

A major policy issue in negotiating international trade policy is the extent to which liberalized access to markets should be preferential and nonreciprocal. Developing countries, through the United Nations Conference on Technology and Development (UNCTAD) and other agencies, have pressed with some success for nonreciprocity, which has become the approved mode of negotiation in the Tokyo round of trade negotiations, and which has already been embodied in the generalized system of preferences created in 1971–72. The demand on the part of less-developed countries for nonreciprocity is motivated, in part, by a sense that past discriminatory trade policies in the advanced countries call for restitution. However, the demand for preferential treatment is based on fallacious mercantilist reasoning and is injurious to the interests of the poor in developing countries. Both advanced and developing countries have an interest in reciprocal, nondiscriminatory trade liberalization.

On a pragmatic level, reciprocal bargaining would result in broader liberalization for exports from less-developed countries, because international trade negotiations are conducted on the basis of mutual, broadly based concessions. Those less-developed countries that have appeared as "free riders" in these negotiations have obtained fewer concessions.

From a welfare standpoint, the reasoning behind the demand for nonreciprocity is fallacious. There would be no long-run welfare cost to the less-developed countries from liberalization of their own markets, especially since they have by no stretch of the imagination any monopsony power in their import markets for manufactures. Widespread overprotection of domestic markets, often through quantitative licensing, has had many ill effects. Substantial windfalls and rents have been created, and much of these have been captured by foreign subsidiaries. Capital-intensive industries using inappropriate technologies have been encouraged and protected. Costs have been raised to export industries and incentives have been biased against protection for foreign markets, limiting the growth of employment. Domestic monopolies and oligopolies have been sheltered against foreign competition. Inward-looking policies are now known to have unfavorable distributional and growth implications.

As in commodity trade, there are substantial mutual gains to be realized from a reciprocal reduction in trade barriers. Since the outcome of this policy is the faster expansion of output and employment in the less-developed countries as compared with the outcome of unilateral or bilateral monopolization of trade, or of the nonreciprocal liberalization of trade, this is the policy approach which has the greatest direct and overall benefits to the world's poor. It should have considerable appeal for advanced countries who are interested in accelerating economic development in the Fourth World through mechanisms which channel additional income directly to the poor.

In summary, the limitation of future population growth demands a rapid fertility decline in the developing countries. Accelerated socioeconomic change among the poor of these countries promotes fertility decline. Increases in income or population growth in the rich countries has little significance and makes little direct contribution to solving the problem of rapid worldwide population growth. Out of their interest in stabilizing world population, the rich countries have, in addition to ethical and political considerations, an additional strong interest in promoting socioeconomc advances among the world's poor. Moreover, even in the means for transferring resources to the developing countries in ways which directly reach the poor, the advanced countries can benefit as well. Because international economic policies which stimulate employment to the greatest extent are those which confer greatest benefits on the world's poor, who are dependent on wage employment and who live in labor-surplus conditions, trade policies which reduce barriers to trade in both rich and poor countries are the most desirable. Financial policies which increase and stabilize the flow of resources to poor countries with a minimum of market interference are the most desirable. Finally, policies in the advanced countries which are more supportive of attempts to redistribute resources within the poor countries are also clearly desirable.

REFERENCES

Beckerman, W., and R. Bacon. 1970. "The International Distribution of Income," in Paul Streeten, ed., *Unfashionable Economics* (London, Weidenfield and Nicolson).

Behrman, Jere. 1977. *International Commoditiy Agreements* (Washington, D.C., Overseas Development Council).

Bhagwati, Jagdish, ed. 1972. *Economics and World Order* (New York, Free Press).

Bogue, Donald. 1969. *Principles of Demography* (Chicago, University of Chicago Press).

Chenery, Hollis, Montek Ahluwalia, Richard Jolly, and John Duloy. 1974. *Redistribution with Growth* (Baltimore, Md., Johns Hopkins University Press for the International Bank for Reconstruction and Development).

Chinn, Dennis. 1977. "Distributional Equality and Economic Growth: The Case of Taiwan," *Economic Development and Cultural Change* vol. 25, no. 1 (October).

Cline, William. 1975. "Distribution and Development: A Survey of Literature," *Journal of Development Economics* vol. 1, no. 4 (February).

Freedman, Ronald. 1960. "Comment," in National Bureau of Economic Research, *Demographic and Economic Change in Developed Countries* (Princeton, N.J., Princeton University Press).

Frejka, Tomas. 1974. *The Future of Population Growth* (New York, Wiley).

Hashimoto, Masanori. 1974. "The Economics of Postwar Fertility in Japan: Differentials and Trends," *Journal Of Political Economy* vol. 82, no. 2, pt. 2 (March/April).

Helleiner, Gerald. 1976. *A World Divided: The Less Developed Countries in the World Economy* (Cambridge, England, Cambridge University Press).

Hughes, Helen. 1975. "Economic Rents, the Distribution of Gains from Mineral Exploitation, and Mineral Development Policy," *World Development* vol. 3, no. 1 (November/December) pp. 811–825.

International Bank for Reconstruction and Development, Development Policy Staff. 1977. *Prospects for Developing Countries, 1978–85* (Washington, D.C., IBRD).

Johnson, Gwendolyn. 1960. "Differential Fertility in European Countries," in National Bureau of Economic Research, *Demographic and Economic Change in Developed Countries* (Princeton, N.J., Princeton University Press).

King, Timothy. 1974. *Population Policies and Economic Development* (Baltimore, The Johns Hopkins University Press for the International Bank for Reconstruction and Development).

Kiser, Clyde. 1960. "Differential Fertility in the United States," in National Bureau of Economic Research, *Demographic and Economic Change in Developed Countries* (Princeton, N.J., Princeton University Press).

Morley, Samuel, and Jeffrey Williamson. 1974. "Demand, Distribution and Employment: The Case of Brazil," *Economic Development and Cultural Change* vol. 23, no. 1 (October).

Ranis, Gustav, and John H. Fei, 1975. "A Model of Growth and Employment in the Open Dualistic Economy: The Case of Korea and Taiwan," *Journal of Development Studies* vol. 11, no. 1 (January) pp. 32–63.

Repetto, Robert. 1972. "Optimal Export Taxes in the Long and Short Run," *Quarterly Journal of Economics,* vol. 86, no. 3 (August).

————. 1978. *Distributional Aspects of North–South Trade and Aid* (Cambridge, Mass., Harvard Center for Population Studies).

Ryder, Norman. 1973. "Recent Trends and Group Differences in Fertility," in Charles Westoff, ed., *Toward the End of Growth* (Englewood, N.J., Prentice Hall).

Schultz, T. Paul. 1974. *Fertility Determinants: A Theory, Evidence, and an Application to Policy Evaluation* (Santa Monica, Calif., Rand Corporation).

Simon, Julian. 1974. *The Effect of Income on Fertility,* Monograph 19, Carolina Population Center (Chapel Hill, N.C., University of North Carolina Press).

Stern, Joseph. 1976. *Growth, Redistribution, and Resource Use* (Cambridge, Mass., Harvard Institute for International Development).

Sweet, James. 1974. "Differentials in the Rate of Fertility Decline, 1960–1970," *Family Planning Perspectives,* vol. 1, no. 2 (Spring) pp. 103–107.

Tabah, Leon. 1971. "Rapport sur les relations entre la fecundité et la condition sociale et economique de la famille en Europe," in Council of Europe, *Second European Population Conference* (Strasbourg, Council of Europe).

United Nations. 1974. *The Population Debate: Materials and Perspectives* (New York, UN).

U.S. Department of Commerce. 1973. *Statistical Abstract of the United States, 1973* (Washington, D.C., GPO).

U.S. Department of State, Agency for International Development. 1974. *Gross National Product, Growth Rate and Trend Data* (Washington, D.C., USAID).

▙ INDEX

THE JOHNS HOPKINS UNIVERSITY PRESS

This book was composed in Linotype Times Roman text and News
Gothic Bold display type by Monotype Composition Company, Inc.
It was printed on 50-lb. Publishers Eggshell Wove paper and bound
in Holliston Roxite cloth by The Maple Press Company.

LIBRARY OF CONGRESS CATALOGING IN PUBLICATION DATA

Repetto, Robert
  Economic equality and fertility in developing countries.

  Includes bibliographical references and index.
    1. Fertility, Human—Economic aspects.   2. Income distribution.
I. Resources for the Future.   II. Title.

HB901.R46   301.32'1   78-20533
ISBN 0-8018-2212-2